THE FIRST PARISH REGISTER

OF THE CHAPEL OF THE CROSS

(1842–1881)

Michael McVaugh, Editor

Chapel Hill, North Carolina

Library of Congress Cataloging-in-Publication Data

Names: McVaugh, M. R. (Michael Rogers), 1938- editor.

Title: The first parish register of the Chapel of the Cross (1842-1881) /

Michael McVaugh, editor.

Description: Chapel Hill, North Carolina : Chapel Hill Historical Society,

[2024] | Includes bibliographical references and index. | Summary: "The

First Parish Register of the Chapel of the Cross is a transcription of

the parish register of the Chapel of the Cross in Chapel Hill, North

Carolina, for the years 1842 to 1881. It includes an Introduction and

bibliography. It is intended as a reference work for church historians,

family historians, and genealogists"-- Provided by publisher.

Identifiers: LCCN 2024017934 | ISBN 9781733854078 (hardcover)

Subjects: LCSH: Chapel of the Cross (Chapel Hill, N.C.)--Registers. |

Chapel of the Cross (Chapel Hill, N.C.)--History. | Episcopal

Church--North Carolina--Chapel Hill--History--19th century. | Chapel

Hill (N.C.)--Church history. | LCGFT: Registers (Lists)

Classification: LCC BX5980.C27 F57 2024 | DDC

283/.856565--dc23/eng/20240513

LC record available at https://lccn.loc.gov/2024017934

Table of Contents

List of Figures

List of Tables

Preface

Upon first entering the Chapel at The Chapel of the Cross, afternoon sunlight filtering through windows catching dust suspended in the air, my eyes flicking from doorway to kneelers to altar, to the gallery where people enslaved once worshipped, I have wondered about who came before us in this physical place. Who came before us in this community of faith, started in the 1840s when Chapel Hill was but a village and the university in its first decades?

Professor Michael McVaugh, archivist of the Chapel of the Cross, has undertaken a labor of love and with the keenly trained eye and mind of a medievalist has delved into the first register of our parish, which records the parish's worshippers and the liturgical acts performed—baptisms, confirmations, marriages, burials. Some individuals have their names recorded; others are recorded as property with the last name of the one who owned them. For some, we can speculate that they wished to participate in these recorded acts. For others, those people held as property, we can only imagine. What did all who worshipped here think, feel, hear, imagine while in the Chapel?

Professor McVaugh has excavated the names of many associated with the parish and traced the threads of how they were connected to one another and to perhaps the town or university. Through the recorded names one receives a glimpse of some of those individuals who worshipped in our parish in its earliest decades. I am grateful to him for his time and efforts for these illuminations. It is my hope that all who worship here will be nourished and spurred to fulfill the mission of the church, to reconcile all things to God, and, as an Easter Vigil prayer reminds us, to "let the whole world see and know that things which were cast down are being raised up, and things which had grown old are being made new [through] Christ our Lord."

The Rev. Elizabeth Marie Melchionna, Rector

Holy Saturday, 2023

The Chapel of the Cross and Its Founders, 1842–1881

From its beginnings, the Episcopal Church has laid down, in the language of its modern canons, that in every parish

> *it shall be the duty of the Rector or Priest-in-Charge to record in the Parish Register all Baptisms, Confirmations, Marriages and Burials.*

Rectors of the Chapel of the Cross in Chapel Hill, North Carolina, have faithfully observed that requirement. Organized in 1842 by the mutual agreement of eighteen local residents who called themselves the Church of the Atonement, its first parish register actually began to record some baptisms in 1845, though it was not given formal parochial status (as the Chapel of the Cross), nor a rector, until 1848; from that point on, the volume contains entries going down with scarcely a break to 1881. This register is a wonderful resource for local history, recording as it does the vital data not only of many Chapel Hill residents, white and black, Episcopalians and non-Episcopalians, but also of university students from across the state who made the church a home while they were in school, and (in 1862–65) of refugee families from eastern North Carolina whose homes and property (enslaved people as well as material goods) were being menaced by Union armies. I hope that making its data available here will be of use to historians and genealogists, but I trust that it can also be of potential interest to Chapel Hillians (and North Carolinians) who want to understand their roots a little better.[1]

With them in mind I am introducing the contents of the register with a short essay that I hope will help interpret its material for the ordinary reader and give it greater meaning. The essay's focus is deliberately local; wider issues in North Carolina or regional history will be visible in the background, but my primary goal has been to explore what this particular document can tell us about life and human relationships in a small southern university village at a time of great change. Occasionally I have passed on contemporary observations from the villagers

---

[1] This introductory essay makes constant reference to the contents of the church register that it discusses, but to direct the reader at every citation to the appropriate page in this edition would swell the volume unnecessarily. It should be possible to find any desired passage mentioning a particular person by consulting the index of names at the end of this volume.

Much incidental biographical detail in this essay has been drawn, also unreferenced, from the US Censuses of 1850 and 1860 and the federal Slave Schedules of the same years, which are easily accessible on line (I myself consulted them through ancestry.com); from *The Alumni History of North Carolina*; and from *The Dictionary of North Carolina Biography*.

themselves (particularly Kemp Plummer Battle and Cornelia Phillips Spencer), but only as tending to illuminate the contents of the register.[2]

I have chosen deliberately to write about our register and its contents in the language of its writer-contributors, as far as convenient, because I am convinced that the unthinking application of modern terminology to describe a society so remote from us in time can risk distorting our attempt to understand it. For example: In the mid-nineteenth-century United States (and well into the twentieth century) a person of African descent was always called "colored"; it is the standard adjective one finds used in letters, books, public documents, speeches by white and black—and throughout our parish register. From the 1960s on, the adjective began increasingly to be felt as offensive, and "black" and then "African-American" came to take its place. But that was not true of the nineteenth century, when it was still a neutral term that black as well as white speakers employed, as for example Frederick Douglass's impassioned speech on "The Future of the Colored Race" (1886) reveals. Consequently, in this introduction to our nineteenth-century parish I use the word "colored" (rather than "black" or "African-American") as a descriptor of individuals who were identified as such in our register or in public documents and who, again like Douglass ("I have spoken as a colored man . . . ," he declaimed, closing a speech of May 1853), no doubt thought of themselves as such. However, if I am writing in my own voice, not specifically about the nineteenth century, I generally use the word "black."

Another terminological policy here should be noted. In the years down to 1865, parishioners often brought "colored" members of their households to church to be baptized, always called "servants" in the register (the word "slave" appears only once in the entire volume), though their enslaved condition was certainly understood. Southern slavery had evolved a functional distinction between two classes of slaves, recognized by masters and slaves alike: field hands, agricultural laborers, who worked and lived apart from their masters, and house servants, who were chosen to live closely with their masters and served their personal needs and wishes.[3]

---

[2] Three people above all have been of great help to me in preparing this essay. Mark Chilton has freely shared with me his unmatched knowledge of Orange County's historical documentation and has supplied unsuspected detail about the lives of many of the individuals mentioned here. Harry Watson's generosity with time and advice has helped me respond to some of the problems that confront the historian of the nineteenth-century South. By patiently correcting my errors of fact, recommending pertinent bibliography, advising me on phraseology, and in many other ways, he has made this a vastly better essay than it would otherwise have been. Whatever defects remain must not be laid to his charge. And in moving my manuscript to the printed page, Tom Jepsen of the Chapel Hill Historical Society has been indispensable—knowledgeable, constructive, and calm.

[3] See the discussion by C. W. Harper, "House Servants and Field Hands: Fragmentation in the Antebellum Slave Community," *North Carolina Historical Review* 55 (1978), 42–59.

The latter were condescendingly imagined by the white world to be the more intelligent, more capable of acquiring cultivation and of developing a personal bond with their owners. The slaves of small Chapel Hill households would all have been of this second kind, and I think it likely that those being presented for baptism were called "servants" by their owners (and the church) to underline their status, and that the word is not simply a genteel euphemism for "slave." I here again follow the register's usage in referring to them individually as "servants," but readers should be clear that, status or no, they were just as much slaves in law as were field hands.

1. Establishing a New Parish

As Archibald Henderson tells it in his history of the Chapel of the Cross (COTC), the seeds of the establishment of an Episcopal parish in Chapel Hill go back to the decision by UNC's president David Swain in 1836 to institute the office of University Chaplain, to be filled in turn by ministers of the four principal Protestant sects. William Mercer Green, who was then the Episcopal rector of St. Matthew's, Hillsborough, was the first to be appointed, and was simultaneously given the position of professor of belles lettres at the university, involving among other things leading two services every Sunday in the university chapel (today's Person Hall), which students had to, and townspeople could, attend. But Professor Elisha Mitchell complained that it would introduce sectarianism into the university if all public services were to be led by the representative of a single sect (Mitchell stood for orthodox Presbyterianism, and gave as an example of sectarianism Green's use of the Lord's Prayer in chapel exercises), and eventually Mitchell and Green were given the responsibility for services on alternate Sundays.

Figure 1. William Mercer Green. From Kemp P. Battle, *History of the University of North Carolina*, Vol. I (Raleigh: Edwards & Broughton, 1907), p. 542.

These tensions between Mitchell and Green continued, and were certainly part of what pushed Green towards the idea of arranging for a separate Episcopal service that would be aimed at university students who wanted it. "Without [the Church], should it be a matter of surprise if their young hearts forget the early lessons of parental love and wander in the ways of sin?" Thus the idea of an Episcopal church in Chapel Hill was born. The parish was canonically organized by twenty-five Chapel Hillians in May 1842, but well before that Green had begun to hold Sunday evening services in a private home (often his own) for students as well as the Episcopal families of the village. It was, after all, UNC students and their spiritual concerns that had been Green's original stimulus.[4]

Green had probably not waited for the formal act of organization to begin arranging for the construction of a church building; he had certainly been seeking subscriptions to that end for some time, some of which had already been paid. In that same month, May 1842, he reported to the diocesan convention that a church was actually under way: "a pleasant, spacious, and convenient lot has been purchased, and a contract made for a good part of the materials for building." During that summer he commissioned plans for the church-to-be from a noted Philadelphia architect, Thomas U. Walter, and no doubt himself took in hand the need to clear the new lot to prepare for the impending construction; he is likely to have used his own slaves to perform the rough labor, and began to accumulate bricks fired in his own kiln to build the walls.[5] By the time of the 1843 convention he was able to report to the convention that "the amount thus far subscribed is about equal to one-half the estimated cost of the building. Nearly all the materials are on the spot, ready for the workman's hand."[6]

Green kept a notebook of subscriptions (and payments) that contains more than 250 entries, made demonstrably as late as 1844 and probably considerably later, totaling slightly less than

---

[4] These paragraphs are based on the account in Archibald Henderson, *The Church of the Atonement and the Chapel of the Cross at Chapel Hill, North Carolina* (Hartford, CT: Church Missions Publishing Company, June–August 1938, 29–36; the quotation is taken from p. 33.

[5] Green certainly owned slaves, for Kemp Battle remarked that "he allowed his slaves to impose on his easy temper, to the indignation of his neighbors" (Battle, *History of the University of North Carolina*, vol. 1, 547); the Greens' servant, "Nanny Green," who attended services with them, appears to have been one such. Battle tells the story that Green's conscientiousness led to his loss of "most of a brick kiln, worth $250, by having the fires extinguished on Saturday night, so as to relieve the laborers from work on Sunday," but does not associate this with the building of the church. Archibald Henderson (*Church of the Atonement*, 36) gives a slightly different description of this event purporting to quote Battle's own words, but I have tried and failed to identify his source, and it may be that Henderson was simply elaborating on the account in Battle's *History*. Henderson adds the details that "through the protracted period of building, Professor Green generously contributed thereto through the labors of several of his slaves and a pair of his mules, . . . 'and [now quoting 'Battle'] the donation of a kiln of bricks prepared for firing on his land and at his expense.'" He then continues with the story of the loss of the kiln. It seems quite possible that the bricks recorded in the *History* as lost were indeed meant for the new church, even though Battle does not say so, and that Henderson introduced these new details to increase the original story's verisimilitude.

[6] Philip A. Rees, "The Chapel of the Cross: An Architectural History" (M.A. thesis, University of North Carolina, 1979), 13.

$4,000.[7] The biggest individual contributions came from a few local Episcopalians: Duncan Cameron, previously Green's parishioner (and patron) in Hillsborough, gave $150 in two installments; the Episcopal members of the UNC faculty—J. DeB. Hooper, Manuel Fetter, W. H. Battle, F. M. Hubbard, J. J. Roberts, Green himself—each pledged and eventually paid from $20 to $100 (David Swain, the University President, pledged $25 but seems never to have paid it). The faculty were of course exceptionally fortunate in enjoying a regular and predictable income, which allowed them to pledge; of the twenty-eight individuals who signed the 1842 document, however, only six seem to have felt able to make a financial commitment to the building of the church. (Battle and Hubbard had not been signers; Anne C. Hall and W. M. Green's son James signed and went on to subscribe.)

The bulk of the donors thus came from the wider diocese, persuaded no doubt by Bishop Ives' regular appeals at Convention; some individuals pledged two or three or even five times. At Edenton in 1844 eight ministers in attendance were moved to promise a total of $300 to the cause, and surely passed on the impulse to their congregations when they went home. Parish organizations took up the appeal: "a few ladies of St. James's Church Wilmington" promised (and paid) $32 "to be expended on furnishing the chancel." The Warrenton congregation took up a collection that brought in $43.81. But what seem to be the last entries in the notebook are for much smaller sums, $2, $3, $5—and they are gifts in cash, not pledges. After several years, the available resources were evidently running low.

And the estimate of cost proved to be unrealistic. The actual work of construction (which began in June 1843) seems to have been carried on by the crews of two local contractors, Isaac Collier of Chapel Hill and mason Dabney Cosby of Hillsborough. The church walls were up by November (though still unwindowed), and apparently the roof followed, but Green wrote a friend sadly in February 1844 that "the workmen recommenced their labors on the church today, but I fear that in a few weeks they must come to a full pause for want of funds." And so it happened. Without money, work stopped, and Green sought further subscriptions, writing mournfully in 1845 that "the rank weed is growing against its windowless walls. The pigeon is building among its rafters."[8] Yet gradually the money crept in. By May 1847 the windows were in place, perhaps made in New York and shipped to North Carolina; by the summer of 1848 it was safe to plaster the interior and to install the pews and altar railing. The consecration of the Chapel of the Cross took place on 19 October 1848. The name of the new parish originally settled on by its organizers in 1842, "The Church of the Atonement," had continued to be used in its reports to the diocese as late as the spring of 1848, but at its October consecration the bishop (Levi Silliman Ives) seems to have insisted on giving it another name, "The Chapel of the Holy Cross"—a choice not perhaps unrelated to his

---

[7] The notebook is in the UNC library, Special Collections: William Mercer Green papers, folder 2.
[8] Rees, "The Chapel of the Cross," 14, 15.

growing sympathy for the Catholic church (which he joined four years later).[9] Bishop Ives still referred to it by that name in his formal report to the diocese in 1849, but the rector's own diocesan report in the same year had already dropped the "Holy"; there it had become simply "The Chapel of the Cross."[10]

The COTC has been fortunate in many of its spiritual leaders, and we frequently illustrate their role in the parish history by celebrating Green's organization of an Episcopal congregation in Chapel Hill, but we fail to appreciate that in fact the early parish had no consistent leadership. Green himself was never formally rector here and left his professorship and Chapel Hill at the end of 1849 to become Bishop of Mississippi. Our first rector, Aaron Olmsted of Connecticut, had been appointed in 1848 but resigned after less than a year in office because (he said) the salary, raised from the congregation, was insufficient.[11] Salary was a persistent problem here, and early rectors who were approached and who came to Chapel Hill did not stay long: Olmsted's successor, Thomas Davis, resigned the position in 1851.

It was only natural that the parish should next have appealed to university faculty to step in; many (like W. M. Green) were ministers as well as educators, they already lived in the village and were known quantities, and they were not unwilling to supplement their university salaries in this way. Thus through most of the 1850s it was a university professor who held the position of rector: Fordyce Hubbard (professor of Latin) in 1851–53, John Thomas Wheat (professor of rhetoric and logic) for much of the rest of the decade;[12] perhaps they were the more willing to take on the responsibility out of solidarity with their colleague Manuel Fetter (professor of Greek), who had been one of the charter members of the original parish and whose family continued to be committed members.[13] Green's vision of a receptive, nurturing Episcopal environment in Chapel Hill for young university students was on its way to realization.[14]

---

[9] Henderson, *Church of the Atonement*, 35.

[10] *Journal of the . . . annual convention of the Protestant Episcopal Church in the state of North Carolina* [hereafter *JPEC*] 33 (1849), 11, 14, 21.

[11] Ibid., 45.

[12] On Hubbard, see Battle, *History*, 1:518; on Wheat, ibid., 1:618.

[13] A portrait of Fetter as university professor is in Battle, *History*, 1: 543–45.

[14] An evocative description of the village as it was in the years around 1850 is in Battle, *History*, 1:607–14.

Figure 2. Fordyce M. Hubbard and John T. Wheat. From Battle, *History of the University of North Carolina,* Vol. I, pp. 542, 684.

We can trace the early history of the parish in some detail because, fortunately for us, the Diocese of North Carolina asked every parish to report annually its number of "communicants," a word that will be an important term for us. It refers to persons who had been admitted to communion, whether as a consequence of confirmation, or on the authority of a priest (in this case, confirmation was anticipated at the bishop's next visit). It was the defining stage in church membership. This report to the May 1858 convention by the rector of St. John's, Fayetteville, sums it up nicely:

> *During the past year the Confirmations have been nearly twice as many, and the additions to the Church by first Communion have been more than twice as many, as those of any previous year of my official connexion with this Parish. The loss by death and removal has also been larger than usual. When it is considered that this Parish is not increasing in population, but the contrary, I have reason to feel encouraged, I think, that I am able to report a net increase in the number of Communicants. I hope, indeed believe, that the work is increasing inwardly also,—that there is a general growth in grace.[15]*

It is apparent that the writer thinks of the "parish" as the geographical entity surrounding Fayetteville, whose inhabitants are of every sect (or none); his own "communicants" are the Episcopal subset of those inhabitants, all made so either by a first communion or by confirmation. As all reporters did, he gave the total number of communicants during the reporting period: "Communicants — Number last year, white 145, colored 15; added by first Communion, white 21, colored 1; ditto by removal, white 1; lost by death, white 5, colored 1; ditto by removal, white 11; total now, white 151, colored 15." In the same issue of the *Journal*, the rector of the Chapel of the Cross reported "Communicants — White, number last year

---

[15] *JPEC* 42 (1858), 43.

43; added by first Communion 3, ditto by removal 5; lost by removal 2; total now, 48."[16] In our own parish register, rectors often drew up a list of communicants in a given year to facilitate reporting, and added to it or noted "removed" in subsequent years to make this report easier to construct; by tracing individual names, we can often determine that an increase in the number of communicants in Chapel Hill in a given year has been brought about by the addition of a dozen or so UNC students there.

Names come and names go, but the successive lists of "communicants" show clearly that there was a core membership of our church that held together throughout those years and through the Civil War, comprising a small set of individuals and their families.

(1) Manuel Fetter (1809–89) was born in Lancaster PA and took the AB and AM degrees from Columbia College (now University) in New York, where he married Sarah Cox. In 1837 he was elected to the chair of ancient languages at UNC and in 1838 was made professor of Greek language and literature at a salary of $1,500 yearly, a position he held until the dismissal of the university faculty thirty years later (see below, p. 35). He was one of the eighteen who signed the organizational statement of the Chapel of the Cross on 13 May 1842, and went on to contribute to it financially.[17] Curiously he never appears on our communicant lists; but his wife and four children were baptized there in the 1840s, and she and several of their children continued as regular communicants. After 1868, when the existing university faculty was forced to resign, he taught in schools in Henderson (NC) and elsewhere.

(2) William Horn Battle (1802–79) graduated from the university in 1820, was admitted to the bar in 1823, and was a prominent lawyer and political figure in the state. He moved from Raleigh to Chapel Hill in 1843 and was professor of law at UNC 1845–68. His family were Baptists, but his wife Lucy M. Plummer (1805–74) was an Episcopalian, and he joined her denomination.[18] In 1845 they arranged for the baptism of their son Kemp Plummer Battle (1831–1919) in our church; after graduating from UNC in 1849, Kemp moved to Raleigh to practice law. The Battle parents and their daughter Susan Catherine (1830–67), however, are all recorded as communicants of the Chapel of the Cross in 1855. In 1868, with the university faculty forced to resign,

---

[16] Ibid., 44. The mistaken addition is in the text as printed.

[17] Fetter's account book for 1841–44 is preserved in the UNC Library. It records (p. 128) a payment of $28.28 on 10 February 1844 to "Wm. M. Green, subscription to the Episcopal Church of this place," and a second (p. 146) of $7.00 on 20 September of the same year to "Mr. Green for P. E. Church of C. Hill."

[18] A brief word portrait is given by his son in Battle, *History*, 1:549; a fuller picture of both his parents is in Kemp Plummer Battle, *Memories of an Old-time Tar Heel* (Chapel Hill: UNC Press, 1945), 12–20.

Judge Battle moved to Raleigh to return to the practice of law, but exceptionally he did not give up his membership in the Chapel Hill church until 1874 and continued to serve repeatedly as one of its delegates (often its only delegate) to diocesan conventions. When his son Kemp was made president of the newly reopened university in 1876, W. H. Battle moved back to Chapel Hill; he, Kemp, and three other members of the family returned to the COTC rolls in 1878.

Figure 3. Core members of the Chapel of the Cross parish. From L to R: Manuel Fetter, William Horn Battle, and Andrew Mickle. Manuel Fetter photo from https://www.ncpedia.org/biography/fetter-manuel. William Horn Battle photo courtesy Anna Kitchin Wilson. Andrew Mickle photo from Town of Chapel Hill.

(3) Another cluster is that of the family of Charles Peter Mallett of Fayetteville. Charles's son Edward (1827–65) entered UNC in 1845, just as Sally Mallett, perhaps his aunt, bought a property in 1845 on what is now Cameron Avenue, which she ran as a boarding house. Edward graduated in 1849 and married Mary Smith Hunter that fall, and on Easter 1851 the couple's son Simmons was baptized at the Chapel of the Cross, with Sally Mallett as a sponsor. Two other Mallett children were baptized there in 1854 and 1856. In the latter year Edward withdrew from the Chapel of the Cross and established himself on a plantation in Craven County, but he enrolled in the Confederate army at the beginning of the Civil War; he was killed at Bentonville in 1865. Meanwhile Edward's older brother William Peter (1819–89), a physician, had come to Chapel Hill in 1856 with his wife Caroline DeBerniere and their two daughters, and their son Thomas was baptized in the church on Easter 1858.[19]

The boys' father, Charles Peter Mallett (1792–1873), had business interests in Fayetteville, but after a failed business venture in New York (1853–56) he and his wife moved to Chapel Hill, perhaps to be closer to their sons, where he established a bookstore. He is on our communicant rolls in 1856 and was a lay reader here in 1858–

---

[19] An appreciation of one aspect of W. P. Mallett's medical practice is "William Peter Mallett," in William de Berniere MacNider, *The Good Doctor* (Chapel Hill: UNC Press, 1953), 102–8.

59;[20] he presented three "coloured children" for baptism in October 1864, and was in church on Easter 1865 when he heard the news that the Yankees were approaching Chapel Hill.[21] By 1860, then, the recorded communicants of the Chapel of the Cross had included Charles Peter Mallett, his wife Sarah, their son Richardson (he would be killed by Confederate deserters in 1863), and their daughter Margaret; William Peter Mallett and his wife Caroline, with their daughter Eliza; Mrs. Frances M. Mallett and her daughter Lissie (Eliza);[22] and Sallie Mallett. They made up a considerable tribe.

(4) Yet another cluster of communicants consists of Andrew Mickle (1815–86), his wife Helen Norwood (1817–92), and their daughters Lizzie B. (1841–86), Annie F. (1847–), Robina N. (1848–1910), and Jane T. (1852–78). Mickle had transferred his membership from Hillsborough to the Chapel of the Cross in October 1849, and he and his wife presented their baby daughter Robina to be baptized there by W. M. Green on Thanksgiving Day of that year (she would be confirmed there in 1864). In the next year's census he described himself as "merchant," and among his concerns in the following decade was a company that he helped incorporate to improve Hillsborough–Chapel Hill communications by the construction of a plank road between them. Mickle might fairly be called an entrepreneur, with wide interests. All his life he enjoyed playing a role in local administration. While living in Hillsborough he had been recorder of deeds for Orange County, from 1835 until his move to Chapel Hill. In the first local election under Reconstruction, after the war, he was elected as clerk of Chapel Hill by the newly appointed township commissioners (1869), and was made its magistrate of police (then the equivalent of mayor) in 1874–75; he was elected bursar of the university in 1875. After Reconstruction Mickle served as Chapel Hill's postmaster from 1877 to 1881.[23]

---

[20] Cf. below, n. 38.

[21] He describes the occupation of Chapel Hill by Union forces in a letter of 18 April 1865 to his son, Charles Beatty Mallett; excerpts from the letter (now in the C. B. Mallett papers, Southern Historical Collection, UNC) can be read in "Documenting the American South," https://docsouth.unc.edu/true/mss06-14/mss06-14.html.

[22] Public records show that Frances [London] Mallett (b. 1806) was married in Wilmington in 1835 to Lallenstedt Mallett of Elizabethtown. How exactly they fit into the Fayetteville family is something of a mystery, but it should be noted that Frances and her daughter are both buried in Fayetteville's Cross Creek cemetery.

[23] Hugh Lefler and Paul Wager, eds., *Orange County—1752–1952* (Chapel Hill: privately published, 1953), 184, 196, 357, 364, 366.

(5) Laura Saunders (1810–81) had married Joseph Hubbard Saunders (UNC '21), who became the Episcopal rector in Pensacola FL. When he died in 1839 she moved with their four children to Raleigh, and from Raleigh to Chapel Hill about 1850; she immediately joined the Chapel of the Cross, returned to it when it was resurrected in the 1870s, and remained a communicant until her death. Her daughter Anne (b. 1837) was confirmed there in 1854, and also remained a communicant. Her son Richard Benbury (1834–90), who married Mary Stenton before 1856, graduated from UNC in 1854 and became a druggist; he was apparently not formally a communicant, but he had his children baptized there in 1860, 1863, 1865, and 1867 (twins). Another son, William Laurence, at least twice stood sponsor at these baptisms.

(6) Mary Ruffin Smith (1804–85) was the oldest child of a prominent Hillsborough figure, James Strudwick Smith; his sons, Frank and Sidney, were difficult and often at odds with one another.[24] Her father saw to it that she was educated in a new school for girls whose superintendent was the young William Mercer Green, rector of the Hillsborough church. In 1834 her father acquired a young slave girl, Harriet, to be Mary's personal servant, but in time first Sidney and then Frank raped Harriet, who bore them four daughters between 1844 and 1852; the mixed-race girls were Mary's property but were raised by her as her nieces. During these latter years James Smith declared bankruptcy while shrewdly sheltering his assets, and built a new home on a plantation in southern Orange County, "Oaklands," where the entire family moved in 1847. Now living near Chapel Hill and its new Episcopal church founded by her admired teacher, Mary Ruffin immediately (1848) became a committed communicant of the Chapel of the Cross. As her enslaved nieces grew up in the ensuing years, she would take them with her in her carriage to Sunday services, and in December 1854 she arranged for their baptism there. Meanwhile her parents had died, her father in 1852 and her mother Delia in 1854; she arranged funerals for both in the new church.[25] She continued to appear on the parish's lists of communicants in 1860 and 1864, and several times in those years brought other slaves to Chapel Hill to be baptized, but she

---

[24] A careful study of Mary Ruffin Smith's life has been published by H. G. Jones, *Miss Mary's Money: Fortune and Misfortune in a North Carolina Plantation Family, 1760–1924* (Jefferson, NC: McFarland, 2015).

[25] Our register records Delia Smith as an 1854 communicant with the added note "first time on her deathbed," and the Hillsborough *Recorder* passed on the same information (Jones, *Miss Mary's Money*, 67). I suspect that her daughter Mary had had a major role in both bringing about the event and then seeing to it that it was known publicly.

was primarily occupied in directing the affairs of the Chatham County plantation during the war.

(7) A final household in the parish needs comment, though it is not easy to summarize its structure. Mrs. Rebecca W. Lucas had probably brought her family to Chapel Hill in the mid-1840s, but the first direct evidence of her presence here comes in 1849. In that year she was reported as a communicant of the COTC, and that December her daughter Frances Lucas ("a lady of this congregation," W. M. Green noted), was married at the COTC to Samuel Field Phillips, a tutor in law at the university. Samuel's father James was the university's professor of mathematics, and Samuel himself went on in time to become Solicitor General of the United States. In the 1850 census we find the young couple living in the home of the groom's brother Charles, an instructor in mathematics, and his wife Laura, W. H. Battle's sister. In that same census Rebecca Lucas reported two more Lucas children still living with her, apparently sons by her second husband, Dr. John Lucas: Samuel (age 26) and Joseph ("school teacher") age 21—the latter seems to be the Joseph Bibb Lucas who attended the university 1845–49 and was appointed tutor in Ancient Languages 1854–57. Joseph was confirmed at the COTC in 1854, and was a regular communicant until his premature death in the summer of 1858. However, Rebecca Lucas had evidently decided to make a home in Chapel Hill for her children by *both* husbands. For also living with Rebecca in that 1850 census was her daughter by her *first* husband (Samuel Garland), Hannah Ryan, as well as three of Hannah's children, David, Garland, and Rebecca. Mother and daughter were regular COTC communicants too, and Mrs. Lucas often appears in our register as sponsor for the baptisms and eventual confirmation of her grandchildren.

These two women, Rebecca Lucas and Mary Ruffin Smith, offer an interesting contrast: Mary Smith propertied and very well-to-do, Rebecca Lucas with certainly far more limited resources; Lucas with ties to the academic side of Chapel Hill life built up through her children, Mary Smith living quite remote from that society. But these very different women were both actively committed to the Chapel of the Cross and to maintaining there the sacramental life of their young dependents, whether free grandchildren or enslaved nieces. Their households, with the others I have mentioned, made up the heart of our church in the 1840s and 1850s—a tiny constant cluster in a small self-contained village.

Occasionally the wider world also found a temporary place in Chapel Hill. In the early 1850s, an important Hillsborough lawyer, planter, and politician, Hugh Waddell, moved his household there. Perhaps it was for family reasons. His oldest son, Henry Marsden Waddell (b. 1828), previously a parishioner at St. Matthew's, married Elizabeth Brownrigg of Columbus (MS) at the Chapel of the Cross in September 1853 and moved his membership there. There too he was baptized, in December of that year, along with his brother, Alfred Moore Waddell

(b. 1834, at that time a student at UNC[26]), with their parents (who had now moved their own membership to the COTC) present at the ceremony; in February 1854 the two brothers were confirmed there by Bishop Thomas Atkinson. By this time Henry had probably informed his parents that Elizabeth was expecting a new little Waddell in September. Their son duly appeared on the 20th of September and was baptized a month later by the rector, John Wheat, with the grandparents in attendance; Hugh Waddell used the occasion to have five of his house servants baptized as well. But the occasion was bittersweet, for the young father had not lived to see his son, having died shortly after his confirmation; his funeral had taken place at the COTC on 21 April. He was buried back in Hillsborough, and the senior Waddells must have returned to that town in the following year, perhaps after the marriage of one of their "servants" (to a servant of Edward Mallett) in September in Chapel Hill, for their names now disappear from the lists of our communicants. With no familial reasons to stay (Alfred had left school without graduating), there was nothing to keep such a figure in a small, self-absorbed village.

Records scattered throughout the register give us a mosaic of what parish life was like in its early days. Attendance at communion, the first Sunday in the month, averaged about 20, and the collection was usually $5 or so in the early 1850s but had risen to almost twice that by 1860.[27] Between 1856 and 1858 the register exceptionally records not only parish income but expenses: the bulk of the latter are regular payments to the parish's unnamed sexton; contributions to a fund for diocesan missions; and books, cards, and shoes for the Sunday school students. Rectorial reports to the annual diocesan conventions suggest that the Sunday school attendees—or "catechumens," as they were more often labeled—had initially numbered about twenty, until Henry T. Lee was chosen as rector in 1856 to relieve the parish's dependence on university faculty. It is probably not coincidence that as soon as Lee arrived the reported size and composition of the Sunday school class changed dramatically, jumping from twenty in 1855 to eighty in his first year, a quarter of them reported to the diocese as "colored." The books he ordered for Sunday school use included two dozen "Catechisms" and one dozen "Oral catechisms"—the latter presumably for teaching the black children, for

---

[26] Alfred Moore Waddell, *Stories of My Life* (Raleigh: Edwards and Broughton, 1908), has little to say about the university of his day and nothing about the members of Chapel of the Cross that he may have known, except unintentionally in an aside: in describing his professors he mentions "the refined and dreamy countenance of Dr. Hubbard, and the courtly grace of Dr. Wheat, and the sensitive diffidence of Dr. Fetter" (26).

[27] Towards the end of the Civil War, in 1864, the parish instituted a new practice of weekly offerings, intended in part to aid "'the families of soldiers in this vicinity'"; E. T. Malone, Jr., *The Episcopal Church in North Carolina During the War Between the States* (Warrenton, NC: Literary Lantern Press, 2013), 20.

since 1830 it had been illegal in North Carolina to teach slaves to read or write.[28] Were the books, and the shoes, part of a plan by the new rector for social amelioration? If so, it seems not to have been successful; in Lee's second year he reported only fifty catechumens, seemingly all white; and after he suddenly left the diocese in 1858 the Sunday school returned to its original size.

One particular ongoing commitment of the parish recorded in our register was recurrent aid and support to a Mrs. Martha Perkins of Chapel Hill, and to her numerous offspring. The 1850 federal census locates her in the Orange County Poor House with two children, Nancy and Andrew. She first appears in the register in 1856, when she and the rector's wife witnessed the baptism of two more of her children: Edward Lazarus, aged 4, who was ill, and Florence Nightingale, just a year old. The next April Mrs. Perkins herself was baptized, and had three further children baptized as well: Andrew (then 12), David (10), and Lucretia (5). In the 1860 census she is enumerated in Chapel Hill as aged 36 with no listed occupation and *seven* children—the above five, as well as Nancy (now aged 16), and Fanny (aged 8). From the moment the parish encountered her, it tried regularly to provide for her: it contributed $1.80 for clothes for Andrew in April 1856; four months later gave Mrs. Perkins $3 for a child's funeral expenses (had Edward died of his illness?) and $2 for herself; in the fall of 1857, $6 for herself, for wood, and for children's clothes, and a further $1.50 for medicines; in 1858, $2.30 for provisions and food. They had become part of the parish. In 1862 Nancy was confirmed, in 1864 Andrew likewise, and both were listed as communicants of the Chapel of the Cross, as their mother had been since 1860. Then they all disappear from the register. One wonders what happened to Mrs. Perkins and her family during and after the war. In 1870 the census indicates that she was still living in Chapel Hill with Fanny and Florence; in 1880 she appears in Pleasant Grove, Alamance Co., living alone, and declaring herself "widowed."

Figure 4. Kemp Plummer Battle. From *History of the University of North Carolina,* Vol. II, frontispiece.

But the congregation quickly came to include more than Chapel Hill residents, for university students were being integrated into this community from the outset. Virtually as soon as the church was completed and consecrated, in 1848, it had an organized choir of which student voices were an essential part. Kemp Plummer Battle, who graduated in 1849 and then moved to Raleigh, has left us this vignette of its earliest days:

---

[28] Guion Griffis Johnson, *Ante-bellum North Carolina: A Social History* (Chapel Hill: UNC Press, 1937), 542–43. Cf. N. Brooks Graebner, "The Episcopal Church and Race in Nineteenth-Century North Carolina," *Anglican and Episcopal History* 78 (March 2009), 85–93, at 89.

Miss Mary W. Green [daughter of W. M. Green] sang with a sweetness and feeling that approached that of stars on the operatic stage. John Manning [UNC '50], afterwards Professor of Law in the University, had an admirable bass, and Richard H. Whitfield [UNC '50; from Demopolis, AL) had the talents needed as conductor of a choir. My sister Susan had a good alto. The first choir known in the Chapel of the Cross was formed, and although I was a very indifferent singer, I was obliged to join in order to escort my sister to and from the meetings, always at night. The leader, supported by no organ or melodeon or piano, used a tuning fork. Notwithstanding this drawback the choir achieved much fame.[29]

Writing of these student singers elsewhere, Battle wrote "I doubt if the Grand Te Deum has ever been more sublimely rendered in North Carolina than by this choir. I remember that Bishop [Levi Silliman] Ives . . . was fervid in his praises."[30]

By 1853, when the parish had achieved a stable rectorate under Fordyce Hubbard, at least thirteen students can be identified as having been a part of its community for a time. Not all students planned, or chose, to stay at the university for four years and receive a degree, and we cannot say how long any of the thirteen were communicants of the parish, but of the ten whose careers I have been able to trace, five received the AB degree and were evidently serious, motivated students—in later life they turned into two lawyers, one physician, and two Episcopal ministers.[31]

In 1854 there was a further sign of success, when Bishop Atkinson came to Chapel Hill for the confirmation of a class presented by the rector, now John T. Wheat. It included five residents of the town, including Sarah Fetter, wife of the professor of Greek; Hugh Waddell's two sons, Alfred and Henry, whom we have encountered coming to Chapel Hill from Hillsborough; and at least three other UNC students: Joseph Bibb Lucas, student in the late 1840s who became a UNC tutor in ancient languages 1854–57; John Snead Hines, who took

---

[29] Battle, *Memories*, 82. Battle went on to identify a further "member of the choir of marked ability who was especially gifted as a wit. His name as a freshman was Johnson De Berniere Mallett [UNC '49], but his aunt, an elderly maid who adopted him, had it changed to Johnson Mallett De Berniere, to win the favor of a bachelor uncle of some wealth." It seems likely that this was the nephew of Sally Mallett; he died in 1851.

[30] Battle, *History*, I:596, where he attributes the organization of the choir to Mary Green: "It was she who organized and trained, so far as I can ascertain, the first church choir in Chapel Hill, in which students were the larger element."

[31] Of these last, Richard Hines '50 became an Episcopal minister in Raleigh; Stephen C. Roberts '52 became an Episcopal minister in Chestertown MD.

his AB here in 1856; and John Huske Tillinghast, a UNC student 1853–54 who went on to take his AB from Hampden Sidney and subsequently became rector of a series of churches in South Carolina. I find it hard to believe that these Episcopal students were socially isolated from the rest of the tiny congregation (Wheat reported a total of 36 communicants to the diocese in 1855); I think everyone would have known one another quite well, older members welcoming new students to their number and wishing them well as they left. Moreover, Episcopal students at the university who had discovered the Chapel of the Cross were bringing their unchurched classmates to it, as Green must have hoped would happen. In October 1858 Edward Hugh Davis (class of 1859) of Elizabeth City was baptized here by John Wheat, sponsored by Walker Anderson ('58) of Wilmington and George Johnston ('59) of Edenton. Davis never finished his degree; he married shortly after this and took his wife home to Elizabeth City, then enlisted in the Confederate army (May 1861) at the beginning of the Civil War. He was soon taken prisoner and released on parole in February 1862, after which he and his wife moved to Chapel Hill to wait the war out. His baptism had evidently "taken," for the couple had two sons baptized in the COTC (in 1862 and 1863) and were listed as communicants when the rector made his report to the diocese in 1864.

In the same month that Hugh Davis was baptized, October 1858, the bishop returned to Chapel Hill for yet another confirmation service: this time the class included two townspeople (a new university professor, Hildreth Hosea Smith, and a "free, coloured woman," Susan Holden) and *fourteen* students! Twelve of them finished their degree in the classes of 1859–61, and one at least went on to become an Episcopal minister.[32] Green's ambition to nurture able young Episcopalians within the university had become an obvious reality under Wheat's guidance. Wheat himself certainly felt gratified by what he had helped to bring about. He reported to the diocese in May 1859 that

> *in October last, I presented a class of sixteen for Confirmation, most of whom were students in the University. These, I am happy to say, have since maintained a consistent walk and conversation amidst the peculiar temptations of College life. They have constantly attended upon the weekly Lecture given for their particular instruction. I have urged upon them the claims of the Ministry and three of them will probably become candidates for orders.[33]*

It would be understandable if the parish community as a whole had begun to feel a certain satisfaction with its first ten years of existence.

But Susan Holden's presence on the list is no less notable, as is her continuing presence on the communicant lists of November 1858 and 1860. The Chapel of the Cross now had its first

---

[32] Augustus Moore Flythe '59 became a minister in Northampton Co.

[33] *JPEC* 43 (1859), 51.

free black member who had joined the congregation by choice, though annual reports make clear that it had long had occasional unfree communicants going back to its organization in the 1840s, probably household servants of white members of the congregation, individuals who were treated as "part of the family," if with a certain inevitable condescension. For example, the one "colored" Chapel Hill communicant reported to the diocese in 1849 was evidently Nanny Green, William Mercer Green's housekeeper; the Green ménage left for Mississippi in December so that he could take up his bishopric there, and in the following year no colored communicants were reported from our church. We know almost nothing about Susan Holden and can only speculate as to what might have brought her here. As we will see, she was widowed when she joined our church. In the federal census of 1860 she is identified as a domestic servant aged 43 living in the Chapel Hill home of Adam and Jane Chavis, "mulattos," but the war and subsequent collapse of the university undoubtedly constricted opportunities in Chapel Hill for blacks as well as for whites, for in 1870 she had moved to Raleigh, now a nurse. In the 1880 census she was in New York City, a servant, and for the first time identified as a widow.

Who were the Chavises with whom she was boarding? The 1860 census identifies Adam as a 28-year-old "teamster," with a wife Jane and a 7-year-old son George.[34] Documents show that he had married Jane Mitchell in Orange County just five years before in a ceremony performed by a Methodist minister, L. S. Burkhead, and it is of real interest that the witness to that ceremony was one J. B. McDade, for in the same 1860 census James B. McDade (appointed Chapel Hill postmaster that year) and his family are found living in Chapel Hill (enumerated in dwelling 110) near the Chavises (in dwelling 121); it suggests a previous acquaintance between the two families. In that same census, Amanda McDade (age 27), evidently James's daughter, is in his household, as is her sister Rose Jeffries aged 32. Rose had married Walter Jeffries in 1850, but her husband had died two years later; his funeral service had been conducted by J. T. Wheat at the Chapel of the Cross. Shortly after that both sisters were confirmed and became regular communicants there, remaining on the communicant lists into the Civil War.

---

[34] It is impossible not to wonder whether Adam Chavis may have been related to John Chavis, conceivably even his grandson. John Chavis (b. 1763) was a free black Virginian, educated at Washington College in Lexington, who came to North Carolina and established a successful and highly esteemed school at Raleigh in 1808, where he taught children of both races (separately) until the mid-1830s; John Hope Franklin called him "the most prominent free Negro in North Carolina." John Chavis married and had at least one son, but little seems to be known of his family: the growing restrictions placed on free blacks by North Carolina laws from the 1830s on has helped hide them from public records. See John Hope Franklin, *The Free Negro in North Carolina, 1790–1860* (Chapel Hill: UNC Press, 1943), 73, 169–74; and Helen Chavis Othow, *John Chavis: African American Patriot, Preacher, Teacher, and Mentor, 1763–1838* (Jefferson, NC: McFarland, 2001).

One more piece of information about the Chavis family should be mentioned: on Easter Day 1856 young George Chavis was baptized at the Chapel of the Cross, with his mother Jane present as a witness.

Are all these cross-connections simply a mass of coincidences? Perhaps; but it does not seem unreasonable to guess that the young women from the McDade household were friendly with the neighboring Chavis household, that their confirmation here in 1853 may have been a factor in both George's baptism here in 1856 and Susan Holden's confirmation here in 1858.[35] In any case, whatever the circumstances that brought Susan Holden to the Chapel of the Cross, we can now appreciate that she knew when she came that she would have at least acquaintances and probably friends there, that her race was not an insurmountable obstacle.[36] Like the parish's appeal to students, one can see her case as a hopeful sign of a potential future.

But circumstances change. Already by the middle of the 1850s John Wheat had begun to feel that "his duties as Professor and Chaplain in the University made it impossible for him to devote to the Parish the time and labor which he thought its importance demanded"[37]—this is what had forced the parish to bring H. T. Lee in as rector. When Lee suddenly left the diocese in early 1858, Wheat agreed reluctantly to act again as rector, but only "pro tem," and only if he could share the responsibilities with his colleague Professor Hubbard.[38] Even this

---

[35] The significance of these actions by the parish is underlined by John Hope Franklin's assessment that "the attitude of the white population in general ... was that the free Negro population was a degraded and despised element in the society of North Carolina; and, as such, it had no place in the ordinary relationships among human beings"; Franklin, *Free Negro*, 189.

[36] The information provided by the COTC register indicates that their motives may have been more complicated than has previously been proposed: "Although segregation in Chapel Hill is not apparent in 1860, there does seem to be clustering of free black families suggestive of a desire for social solidarity and mutual support. . . . The largest cluster of black families included thirty-three-year-old Susan Bishop and her four children, fifty-five-year-old Millie Walker, forty-five-year-old Adeline Mitchell and her three young children, and twenty-eight-year-old Adam Chavis and his wife and child, along with forty-three-year-old Susan Holden and eight-year-old Lizzie Archer. Only Chavis, a teamster, and Susan Holden, a domestic servant, had occupations listed in the census, while three single women were living with children. Thus, it may very well be that this cluster was based, in part, on black women joining together for mutual support and survival"; John K. (Yonni) Chapman, "Black Freedom and the University of North Carolina, 1793–1960" (PhD diss., UNC, 2006), p. 31; accessed at http://webcat.lib.unc.edu/search?/aChapman%2C+John+K/achapman+john+k/1%2C2%2C4%2CB/frames et&FF=achapman+john+kenyon&2%2C%2C3, where the pagination is changed from the original in the University of North Carolina Library.

[37] *JPEC* 40 (1856), 22.

[38] Wheat made it clear to the Convention that he was reporting merely as a professor in the university, not as rector: "During the past year, besides my duties as a Professor and Chaplain in the State University,

kept him too busy, however: in June 1859 he resigned his position as university professor and moved to take a large parish in Little Rock, leaving the leadership of the parish once again in doubt just on the eve of the Civil War.

2. White and Black in Chapel Hill in 1860

What was Chapel Hill like at that pregnant moment? In 1860 the white population of Orange County (it then included a large portion of today's Durham County, which was only created in 1881) was 11,311; the county also held 528 free blacks and 5,108 slaves.[39] The census returns for that year indicate that the free population of Chapel Hill itself was about 1,440, and the federal Slave Schedules (a separate section of the federal censuses of 1850 and 1860) show that 72 of them were slave-holders. Most individuals in Chapel Hill thus did not own slaves, and this was true of North Carolina in general; in that same census year only 28 percent of the state's citizens owned one or more slaves.[40] Those 72 slave-holders owned 480 slaves among themselves, but they were not equally distributed: 260 slaves, more than half, were owned by just nine people, who held between 18 and 50 slaves each, a size that one historian has taken to represent a "plantation household" and amounting to a very large investment.[41] Thus the other 63 Chapel Hillians owned 220 slaves, 4 each on average.

Those Chapel Hillians who owned 40 or 50 slaves would have had big farms or plantations in southern and eastern Orange County (extending, of course, into present-day Durham County) that needed a large labor force. The situation was quite otherwise in the tiny village of Chapel Hill proper, where slaves were used to keep house for the families of university professors and of local merchants, and we can see this reflected in the households of COTC communicants based in Chapel Hill (some of course lived in Hillsborough or Durham). In the Slave Schedules of 1860 only 5 of the 56 Chapel Hill communicants are recorded as owning slaves: the physician W. P. Mallett owned 12; Professor Manuel Fetter also 12; the merchant Andrew Mickle 6; Professor Hildreth Smith 4; and Sally Mallett (who operated a boarding house on what is now Cameron Avenue), 3. The impression given by these absolute numbers is perhaps

---

I have served, (part of the time alternately with Professor Hubbard and in conjunction with Mr. Chas. P. Mallett, acting most acceptably as Lay Reader,) in the vacant Parish of the Chapel of the Cross at Chapel Hill"; *JPEC* 43 (1859), 51.

[39] Lefler and Wager, *Orange County*, 96.

[40] Johnson, *Ante-bellum*, 469.

[41] Elizabeth Fox-Genovese, *Within the Plantation Household: Black and White Women of the Old South* (Chapel Hill: UNC Press, 1988), 41.

misleading, because they clearly include families and hence large numbers of the elderly and children who were not a significant part of a domestic work force (the Slave Schedules report every slave's age and sex, though not name). Fetter's dozen enumerated slaves included a woman aged 70 and a man and a woman aged respectively 40 and 24, as well as children of 10, 8, 8, 6, 6, 4, 3, 1 , and ½ years. Sally Mallett's slaves were a couple, both aged 55, and a ten-year-old girl. Mickle's included three young women in their twenties (did they serve in his shop as well as his home?) and three girls under ten. W. P. Mallett owned a couple in their fifties, but also six young children from 12 to less than a year of age. Smith owned a 58-year-old woman, a boy and a girl in their mid-teens, and a one-year-old boy. In this regard William Horn Battle was, as in many other respects, an atypical figure. Appointed professor of law at the university in 1845, he maintained a home in Chapel Hill (rebuilt by his son Kemp, who named it "Senlac"[42]), but in 1860 his residence for census purposes (and that of his wife and four of his children) was a property in Orange County and not in Chapel Hill proper, rather in "Durhamsville" on the south side of the NC railroad; he owned 18 slaves, 6 of whom were adults (apparently including two married couples) and the rest aged between 15 and 2.

The patterns of slave life on the large Southern plantations, its supervision and control, can be reconstructed from the records that owners routinely kept, and the dynamics of the "plantation household" can be assessed by studying what one historian has called "a very special universe of introspective women whose papers have survived,"[43] the writings left by white women who supervised the actions of the many slaves who operated their masters' households and made their lives more comfortable—that is, the house servants, as distinct from the field hands. The perception of a difference between the two in status as well as circumstance was early recognized both by slaves and by masters, and the label of "servants" that was applied routinely to the former group in antebellum North Carolina was not so much a euphemism as it was a recognition of their superior status.[44]

However, what the dynamics were between one or two "servants" and their masters in a small village household is much harder to recover, and vastly more difficult to generalize about. Plantation owners throughout the south shared a broadly common class and its values, and a common concern with profitable agricultural production. But the merchants, craftsmen, laborers, and small farmers who made up a village had different values, and probably different backgrounds, that enhance the individuality of each particular case. And the academic

---

[42] He named it after the famous "battle" of 1066. Today it is owned by the Carolina Christian Study Center, Inc.

[43] Fox-Genovese, *Within*, 42.

[44] Harper, "House Servants and Field Hands."

environment must have made the dynamics between servants and master in Chapel Hill households highly variable, and unlike those anywhere else in the state, for in the 1850s the majority of the University's 9 senior faculty had been brought up and educated outside the South and had subsequently had to come to terms with, indeed to govern a household in, a slave-based society: Elisha Mitchell (Yale, AB 1813; Chemistry); James Phillips (privately educated in England; Mathematics); Fordyce Hubbard (Williams, AB 1829; Latin); Manuel Fetter (Columbia, AB, ca. 1834; Greek); H. H. Smith (Bowdoin, AB 1842; Foreign languages).[45] They could scarcely avoid bringing their cultural formation with them to North Carolina—but did it retain the power to affect their behavior in a new society?

We are fortunate to have frequent inner glimpses of the household of one of these men. James Phillips (1792–1867) came to New York in 1818 from Plymouth (England), where his father was an Anglican priest. He married in 1821, and in 1826, now with three children, the couple moved to Chapel Hill, where Phillips became professor of mathematics at the university.[46] Soon after coming to Chapel Hill Phillips bought two slaves to operate his household, a couple named Ben and Dilsey. The couple were fixtures in the home as the three children grew up. Ben, for whatever reason, does not appear in the Slave Schedules of 1860, but Dilsey is still there (not of course identified by name), a female aged 60. In the early 1830s Phillips became converted to a fervent Presbyterianism, and in 1833 he was licensed to preach. In reaction to recent state legislation prohibiting black preachers from leading worship, he built a shed behind his house, where he could hold services for blacks, preaching to them on Sunday afternoons and gaining a considerable audience. We can probably presume that Ben and Dilsey were among them.

The Phillips' daughter Cornelia (b. 1825) was an indefatigable writer all her life, and her correspondence with friends and family, as well as her regular contributions to newspapers, gives unmatched pictures of life in nineteenth-century Chapel Hill and of her own household in particular. Thus, reminiscing on these pre-war years, she describes "Summer vacation times in Chapel Hill in the Forties! All of us sweetly doing nothing through the long hot days— going to the University Library, and bringing home lots of books, . . . lying down after dinner to read. Going out later to find our Aunt Dilsey sitting at her cabin door smoking her pipe—

---

[45] Albert Shipp (History), William H. Battle (Law), and James Phillips' son Charles (Civil Engineering) all graduated from UNC, and John Wheat (Rhetoric and Logic) from Virginia Theological Seminary.

[46] Annette C. Wright, "The 'Grown-up Daughter': The Case of North Carolina's Cornelia Phillips Spencer," *The North Carolina Historical Review* 74 (1997), 260–83, offers an analysis of Cornelia's character and attitudes against the background of her family. But the analysis rests entirely on Cornelia's many writings published in later life in obvious reaction to the Civil War and its consequences; Wright has no evidence to offer and nothing to say about the *pre-war* Cornelia that might illuminate the broader argument I am making here.

perhaps patching something for Uncle Ben. . . . Lotos eaters we were in those Forties and Fifties." In 1860, newly married, she wrote from Alabama to a young niece, pretending to speak in the voice of her new baby: "And tell Aunt Dilsey I love her right now, because my Mama loves her. She has got to love me when I come, and you must love me, all of you, when I come, and I'm coming!"[47] Cornelia's early letters suggest real affection for Dilsey, something approaching family feeling, if tinged inevitably with a certain paternalism.

The Civil War and its outcome of course had a great effect on individual attitudes, exposing or strengthening latent tendencies. It made Cornelia Phillips (now Spencer) into an acerbic political conservative, with a more pronounced racial paternalism that nevertheless left her obvious affection for Dilsey unchanged, but in contrast it developed her older brother Samuel into an outspoken and exceptionally vigorous exponent of civil rights for the newly freed blacks at the state and national level. (Their brother Charles became a Presbyterian minister like their father, and was pastor of Chapel Hill's Presbyterian church 1857–68; he also had become professor of civil engineering and mathematics at UNC.) Despite political differences, Samuel and Cornelia remained very close in many of their views, united by their common upbringing. In a letter to their niece on the occasion of her mother's death, in February 1881, she wrote: "For the funeral we did not send a paper or funeral notice round. When I got home from the church, walking with Uncle Sam, there was dear old Aunt Dilsey sitting by the fire. [After emancipation Dilsey had moved out of Chapel Hill to a cabin on the Eno River.] Uncle Sam said to her that he thought so much of her, for coming and staying with us!"[48] The mutual affection was real, and the paternalism much diminished. To what extent the children were shaped by James Phillips's example remains an open question.

---

[47] Hope Summerell Chamberlain, *Old Days in Chapel Hill* (Chapel Hill: UNC Press, 1926), 35, 67.

[48] On 25 May 1894 she recorded Dilsey's death that day in her private journal: ". . . faithful servant in our family for about sixty years. I suppose her to have been about 92 or 93 years old. In face and person she bore the appearance of extreme old age. She died after a tedious illness, in full possession of her senses, her characteristic good nature, good sense, dignity, loyalty, and unshaken faith in her Redeemer. . . . She was twelve years old when the Old South Building was being erected, and liked to tell that she had turned the grindstone on which the workmen sharpened their tools"; Ibid., 259, 300.

Figure 5. Cornelia Phillips Spencer. From Battle, *History of the University of North Carolina,* Vol. II, p. 96.

Three of these faculty immigrants from the North, as it happens, were Episcopalians and communicants of the COTC, and we can continue by trying to recover their experience. Hildreth Smith joined the faculty only in 1858, and almost nothing is known of his life in Chapel Hill; more is known of Fordyce Hubbard, our intermittent rector but a regular communicant. Born in Massachusetts, after taking his degree from Williams College he had married, had a daughter, and taught Latin for some years; then in 1842 he was ordained and was made rector of Christ Church, New Bern, for a time, before going on to direct a high school in Wake County. In 1848 he accepted the professorship of Latin at UNC and remained there for twenty years.[49] He thus lived in North Carolina for nearly three decades, yet as far as can be told he never owned slaves; he is not to be found in the Slave Schedules of 1850 or 1860. The 1860 census shows him, his wife, and his daughter, heading a household that also included a white twenty-seven-year-old master mechanic, his young wife and small child; another fifteen-year-old white female; and four plasterers and a painter, the last all black men in their twenties. A recent UNC dissertation used Hubbard's case to demonstrate how whites and African-Americans might live in the same Chapel Hill household during the antebellum years, without giving any attention to his particular background;[50] but is it not conceivable that his behavior was to some extent the product of his early upbringing?

From the third COTC member, Manuel Fetter, an account book survives for the years 1841–44, shortly after he and his wife Sarah had left New York to settle in Chapel Hill (1838–39), and in revealing how he spent his money it gives us a few hints about *his* household in his early years in the South.[51] As the book opens in 1841, we find Fetter recording scattered small payments to "Solomon," "Tony," and the like for making purchases for him—probably slaves

---

[49] Cornelia Phillips Spencer, who seldom restrained an acerbic tongue, named Hubbard one of the three faculty members who "did more by their intercourse with the students, by their conversation and style of learning, to give them scholarly tastes, elevate their aims, and inspire them to generous ambition"; in "Pen and Ink Sketches of the U.N.C." (typewritten copy of articles in the Raleigh *Sentinel,* 1869), Special Collections, Wilson Library, University of North Carolina.

[50] Chapman, "Black Freedom and the University," 30.

[51] The manuscript book is preserved in Special Collections, Wilson Library, University of North Carolina. It is inscribed "Book C," and at its end refers the reader to "Book D." Because its entries are arranged chronologically within a month, and it gives one month to each successive page, it will be easy to find there the events I cite, and in most cases I have not bothered to record their precise pagination.

whom their owners allowed to present themselves for hire.[52] Others he hired to work by the day or week —"Edmund (black)" was hired to work in the garden at 40 cents a day on three occasions totaling ten days in March 1841. He also hired from Elisha Mitchell the latter's slave "Phyllis (colored)" to work for him on a yearly basis from 1840 (and perhaps before) to at least 1844, when the account book closes.[53] Phyllis's help may have been sought as support for Sarah. A first child (Frederick) had been born to the Fetters the year after they came to Chapel Hill, a second (William) had arrived in 1841 and a third (Henry) appeared in 1843; in January 1844 Phyllis was paid a small sum "for drawing Sarah's breasts." By 1850 there would be six young Fetters.

The steady growth of household responsibilities may help explain why in the fall of 1841 Fetter bought two slaves of his own, "Ben" (for $139) and "Serina" (for $350); their roles in the household are never specified, but during 1841–42 he regularly made small gifts of money to each of them from time to time, and a further gift at Christmas 1841. Ben last appears in the accounts in July 1842, and may soon have died, for shortly thereafter we find Fetter beginning again to pay a number of individuals to carry out purchases for him. Beginning in January 1843 he started entrusting numerous small commissions to one person in particular, "Stephen (Negro)," and two months later he bought Stephen from his owner for the considerable sum of $486. Stephen seems to have taken Ben's place in the household. From then on he was entrusted with more and more important assignments and was paid cash for each; separate gifts of money to Stephen's mother ("old Bec") in August and at Christmas 1843 were presumably meant as further rewards to him. He seems to have become a kind of major-domo in the Fetter household by the time this volume closes in December 1844. Stephen was also making and repairing shoes for members of the household, not only for Serina but for the Fetters' own young sons, Fred and Will, and he was paid in each individual case for his work.[54] Readers can decide for themselves whether this brief look at a very small and constricted portion of Fetter's household is at all meaningful, so early in his life in the South; but it can certainly be read as revealing a man who was more comfortable in making use of money to pay for or recognize service, than in simply enforcing service as an inherent obligation of bondage.

---

[52] Thus "Mrs. Winfree's Tony" worked a number of days for Fetter (at $.25 a day) in 1842: "Book C," 70, 74, 80.

[53] Ibid., 36, 48, 120.

[54] "Stephen in full for making 2 pr. shoes $1.00" ("Book C," 114); "Stephen for soling Will's shoes $.15" (122); "Stephen for soling Fred's shoes $.15" (130); "Stephen for mending shoes for Rina $.35" (150).

All these men, moving to the South, would have needed somehow to reconcile their sense of personal integrity with their sudden incorporation into a society pervaded by the cruelty of enslavement. James Phillips kept few slaves and seems to have acknowledged their autonomy and needs. Manuel Fetter eventually accepted slavery into his household while apparently trying to disguise or temper its harshness;[55] Fordyce Hubbard seems to have managed to stay aloof from direct involvement with enslavement. But none could have failed to recognize uncomfortably that whatever they might do personally, the smooth course of their own lives was made possible only by the brutality of their society's institutions. It is of course more difficult to generalize about prewar Northern attitudes toward slavery than about Southern ones. Professor Elisha Mitchell came from Yale to teach at UNC in 1818, and the scriptural literalness of his conservative Presbyterianism made him a vigorous defender of slavery until his death in 1857. And we will soon meet Francis Hilliard of Lowell MA, a leading scholar in Harvard's class of 1852 and COTC's temporary rector during the Civil War, whose commitment to the culture and institutions of the South, including the enslavement of Africans, began while he was still in college. Thus little can be made of the cases described above. But they certainly do not invalidate the possibility that some of the pre-war households of Chapel Hill academics raised in the north might have been loci of relatively "liberal" attitudes, which found expression in varying degrees in members of the family as time went on, as children matured, and as events changed the wider society.

If the private feelings and attitudes of individual parishioners on race relations are largely hidden from us, the behavior of the parish as a whole has left us traces to study, though what they mean is open to debate. There was a strong movement in antebellum North Carolina towards slave evangelization, encouraging the Christianization of slaves through baptism and through religious education. Brooks Graebner has suggested that bishops and leaders of the clergy endorsed it because it could be promoted without attacking the practice of slavery itself; it preached benevolence but did not challenge control.[56] William Mercer Green had early been

---

[55] A more direct indication that Fetter was conscious of slavery as a social evil and looked for ways to eradicate it is his support of the American Colonization Society, which focused on purchasing and freeing slaves and paying their passage to the new country of Liberia on the west coast of Africa; his accounts record a donation to the Society in August 1842. In the end it proved an unrealistic project, but it was nevertheless the only alternative widely proposed to immediate emancipation (which seemed even more unrealistic). It is not generally known that UNC's first president, Joseph Caldwell (Princeton '91), had been a very early (1825–1829) supporter of the Society (*African Repository*, 1:159, 161, 2:32).

[56] N. Brooks Graebner, "'Hitherto excluded for want of room': Slave evangelization in the North Carolina ministry of William Mercer Green from 1823 to 1848," paper presented to the Natchez Historical Association, October 9, 2009. The paper has almost nothing to say about Green in the Chapel Hill of the 1840s, merely claiming Green's indirect influence on Mary Ruffin Smith's continuing care for her nieces: "The presence of these children in a gallery built by William Mercer Green, sent there by a pupil and parishioner of William Mercer Green, and accompanied to church by a close associate and friend of

an earnest supporter of slave evangelization, and was noted for his efforts in this regard while rector of St. Matthew's, Hillsborough, both within the parish (where he added a slave gallery to the church) and on the nearby plantation of Duncan Cameron, where he taught and preached to slaves. His subsequent incorporation of a similar gallery in the Chapel of the Cross suggests that he was still a supporter of such a policy, and the same seems clear even earlier, for already in 1844, long before a physical church existed, our register records:

> *Mary Ann (coloured child) daughter of Jane & [blank] and belonging to Dr. George Moore. baptized Dec. 8th 1844 by Rev. W. M. Green. Billy Waddell (coloured) Sponsor.*

Mary Ann is the only colored Chapel Hill child Green is recorded as having baptized before he moved to Mississippi to take up its bishopric; but in the 1840s and 1850s, the few slave-holding communicants in the parish who had known Green personally (like George Moore, who had signed the founding document of 1842)[57] adhered intermittently to this practice: the Battle family presented seven servants to be baptized, the Malletts seven, Manuel Fetter one, and Andrew Mickle three. In all, in the period 1845–60 there were 35 slave baptisms and 75 white baptisms in our parish. At the personal level, benevolence seems perhaps no less likely a motive for these baptisms than control.

One example will show how much and yet how little evidence we have about these "servants" baptized in our church. In 1850 Andrew Mickle was recorded in the federal Slave Schedules as owning one male slave aged 12 and four females aged 9, 20, 25, and 55. Our parish register shows that in 1854 he provided for the baptism of a three-year-old "servant" girl, Amy, on the same occasion that his own two-month-old son Andrew was baptized; in 1859 he and his wife were sponsors at the baptism of another "colored servant," Sylvia, whose age is not mentioned. Then in the Slave Schedules of 1860 he reported owning 3 females aged 1, 3, and 9, and three females aged between 21 and 27. Amy might be the nine-year-old of the 1860 schedule, but what of the other two little girls? might Sylvia have been the three-year-old? In which case, did Mickle choose not to baptize the third, or had he not yet arranged for it? There is really no way of deciding from the available evidence how seriously or how consistently he felt a responsibility for the baptism of the black children he owned. In the 1870 census Amy Mickle does not appear, but Sylvia Mickle ("mulatto, age 12") and Lucy Mickle ("mulatto, age 30, cook") are both found living on an Orange County farm. Might not Lucy have been the

---

William Mercer Green, is perhaps the greatest direct [*sic*!] evidence of the lasting impact of Green's own commitment to slave evangelization" (11). See also N. Brooks Graebner, "The Episcopal Church and Race in Nineteenth-Century North Carolina," *Anglican and Episcopal History* 78 (2009), 85–93.

[57] A brief sketch of Dr. George Moore is in Battle, *History*, 1:609.

21-year-old of the 1860 schedule, and Sylvia her daughter? Such data may be meat and drink to the genealogist, but they are of little use to the parish historian.

3. The COTC in the Civil War and Its Immediate Aftermath

John Brown's raid on Harper's Ferry in October 1859 and Lincoln's election as president the next fall led to the secession of the southern states in 1861 and the outbreak of the Civil War. The years that followed were painful in innumerable ways for our parish. Young North Carolinians (like Hugh Davis) had other things to think about than a UNC degree, and Chapel Hill admissions shrank. After that confirmation service of 1858, only five more Carolina students joined the Chapel of the Cross, and three of them had entered the university before the war had alerted young men to other priorities. The other two enrolled much later, in the class of 1865, both aiming at admission into the Episcopal ministry outside the south—they ended up in New York and Montana. The early infusion of student youth and energy into our parish had come to a stop with the onset of war.

And naturally the course of the war between 1861 and 1865 meant that the shrunken parish began to hear repeatedly of the deaths of earlier students it had known closely, and cared for. Benjamin Huske, whom old-timers would have remembered as part of the very first student cluster in 1841, died of wounds received at Seven Pines in 1862, but more recent congregants were dying too. Hugh Davis's two baptismal sponsors both died, George Johnston in 1862 from battle wounds, Walker Anderson at the battle of the Wilderness in 1864. Of those fourteen confirmands in 1858, thirteen joined the Confederate army after war broke out, and three of them died young as a result: Laurence Anderson at Shiloh in 1862, George Martin from battle wounds in 1863, George Bryan at Charles City Roads in 1864. Worse still, parishioners had to agonize about the prospects for their own small continuing community, which included two young men of military age: John Wheat, Jr. (born in 1830), the son of the rector, and Frederic Fetter (born in 1838), the son of Manuel and Sarah Fetter. They had grown up together, they had both been communicants of the church, and they both enlisted at the beginning of the war. It was not long before the news came that John had been among those killed at Shiloh; what might happen to Frederic? Indeed, with no resources, weakened ties to a university that was itself in serious financial difficulties, and above all, with no stable leadership, what might happen to the parish? It had not been at all easy in peacetime to find a rector who could understand and lead this unique community; in wartime, what hope was there of finding such a rector?

In the end, John Thomas Wheat was succeeded as rector by Francis Hilliard, and it was the latter who directed our parish all through the Civil War. Hilliard had a very different orientation from the professors who had preceded him in the role of rector. Born in Lowell

MA in 1832, he went to Harvard and was one of the best scholars in the class of 1852.[58] At college he became the intimate friend of Josiah Collins IV, the heir to Somerset Place—the greatest plantation in North Carolina's Washington County, where 4,000 acres were worked by more than 300 slaves—and he came fully to share his friend's fervent commitment to the South and its society. Upon his graduation Hilliard came to Somerset Place to live, and stayed there for two years as tutor to Josiah's younger siblings. Subsequently, after preparation at General Theological Seminary in New York, he returned to North Carolina for his ordination to the diaconate in 1856 and was made assistant to Samuel Iredell Johnston, rector of St. Paul's, Edenton. He married Johnston's daughter in 1857, and in 1859 was installed as rector at Grace Church, Plymouth, just thirty miles from his friend at Somerset Place, at almost exactly the moment when Wheat was resigning from UNC and leaving the Chapel of the Cross without a rector. Yet two years later, only a few weeks after the beginning of the war in April, Hilliard resigned his post at Plymouth for "motives both of private and public obligation" to come abruptly as rector to Chapel Hill.[59] It must have been hard for our parish to turn for its leadership to someone who knew nothing of W. M. Green, nothing of its past and traditions, nothing of the University of North Carolina and its students—nothing of the Piedmont, rather imbued with admiration for the society of the coastal plain—but as the war broke out there can have been no other options open to it.

Figure 6. Francis M. Hilliard. From Grace Williamson Edes, *Annals of the Harvard College Class of 1852* (Cambridge, MA, 1922), p. 92.

How Hilliard had learned that there was a vacancy at Chapel Hill is unclear, but it may be that he came to hear of it through his close friendship with Josiah Collins. After John Wheat had left, the vestry had arranged with E. M. Forbes, rector at Elizabeth City, to serve the Chapel of the Cross temporarily, and notes in our register show that Forbes was active here from at least August 1859 to October 1860, but he must have left thereafter to return to his home parish. It could be that Forbes was the informant; he knew the Collins family well, having lived and preached at Somerset Place in the late 1830s,[60] and could have mentioned to Josiah that there

---

[58] Grace Williamson Edes, *Annals of the Harvard College Class of 1852* (Cambridge, MA: privately printed, 1922), 61–62 (Collins), 101–2 (Hilliard).

[59] *JPEC* 45 (1861), 36. It is an ironic coincidence that Hilliard's report for the parish he had left is followed in this issue of the *Journal* by his report for the parish to which he had moved.

[60] "In 1836 [Josiah Collins III] erected a chapel on the plantation and engaged E. M. Forbes to convert the slaves from Methodism to his own Episcopal Church, a three-year process"; *Dictionary of North Carolina Biography*, 1:405. Only a few years later he would make the first—and single largest ($200)—pledge to the construction of the Chapel of the Cross that W. M. Green recorded. See also Laurence Foushee

was now a vacancy here. Or Josiah could have learned of it from his wife's family, who were wealthy planters in Hillsborough, and mentioned it to Hilliard. Whatever the sequence of events, by June 1861 Hilliard was baptizing an infant at the Chapel of the Cross, 150 miles away from his former parish in Plymouth.

Hilliard's various connections with the wealthy aristocracy of eastern North Carolina helped make Chapel Hill seem an attractive refuge as the war came to their part of the state. The earliest of these was his father-in-law, Samuel I. Johnston, who we know left Edenton early in 1862 with his large household—in 1860, five children and thirteen slaves—and joined Hilliard in Chapel Hill, just as Union troops were beginning to occupy large portions of the coastal counties.[61] Thereafter the influx was constant, and hard to keep up with. In 1864 Hilliard drew up what seems to be a list of the new members of the congregation, who appear to have come from all over eastern North Carolina; it included Joseph H. Pool (of Elizabeth City, which was occupied by Union forces in February 1862; 57 slaves in 1860); Mrs. H. G. Spruill and her daughter Eveline (of Plymouth, occupied by Union forces in May 1862; 18 slaves); Dr. Moses John de Rossett and his wife Ada (members of a leading Wilmington family); and several others.

All these refugees disappear from our church register after the war and presumably returned home. The rector himself, the Rev. Mr. Hilliard, did just this. He remained in Chapel Hill through the war years, except for the period September 1862–February 1863, when he served as a chaplain with the Confederate army.[62] But three months after the final surrender of Confederate forces ensured that the fighting was over, in July 1865, he resigned his rectorship

London and Sarah McCulloh Lemmon, eds., *The Episcopal Church in North Carolina, 1701–1959* (Raleigh, NC: The Episcopal Diocese of North Carolina, 1987), 190–91.

[61] There are reasons to think that Johnston's flight from Edenton to Chapel Hill was triggered by the Union capture of Roanoke Island in mid-February 1862, which opened up interior port cities to invasion; London and Lemmon, *Episcopal Church,* 248.

[62] "For nearly six months of the past Conventional year, from the first of September to about the middle of February, I was absent from the Parish, having accepted an appointment as Chaplain in the army of the Confederate States, and being stationed, for the most part during that time, as Post Chaplain at Wilmington and points below on the Cape Fear River. Meantime the Parish was most faithfully and acceptably served by the Rev. J. H. Wingfield, Rector of Trinity Church, Portsmouth, Va., who has also, both before my absence and since my return, rendered me constant and valuable assistance"; *JPEC* 47 (1863), 45. Curiously, our register shows that Hilliard baptized a child at the Chapel of the Cross on 6 October 1863; perhaps he had leave from the army to return here briefly. The Rev. J. H. Wingfield was evidently another refugee in Chapel Hill, for Portsmouth had been occupied by Union forces in May 1862. In Hilliard's absence, Wingfield celebrated the marriage of Edward Hines and Louisa Pool in our church but neglected to enter the date; other records reveal that it took place on 16 September 1863.

and with his relatives returned circuitously to Edenton, eventually becoming rector of St. Paul's there (his father-in-law had died shortly before the war's end).

Unfortunately for today's parish historian, the continuous arrival of families from eastern North Carolina throughout the war made it virtually impossible for Hilliard to report accurately on his congregation's size. The actual lists of communicants he drew up during the war are repetitious and confusing, and he obviously had difficulty each year in deciding which persons should be identified as such.[63] But the figures that he settled on and reported tell the broad story: there were twice as many Episcopal communicants here in May 1863 as there had been in 1860 (see Table 1). Another statistic hinting at how the Chapel of the Cross— and Chapel Hill—was changing during the war is the surge in the number of "catechumens," children both white and black, that Hilliard reported to the convention in successive years. The number of white catechumens continued at the level that had been the norm during the previous twenty years, two dozen or so every year, but the number of black catechumens grew to two or three times that, to as many as seventy-five in 1862! It seems likely that this testifies to the presence in Chapel Hill of large numbers of household slaves of the plantation families from the coast, brought with them by their owners in their relocation.

---

[63] "Among the Communicants above reported are several who have removed to Chapel Hill on account of the actual or threatened occupation of their homes by our country's enemies. It has been thought proper to include them here, as, in most cases, no report was likely to be made from the Parishes to which they properly belonged"; *JPEC* 46 (1862), 46. The diocesan convention to which he was reporting was meeting in Chapel Hill itself. In the following year Hilliard apologized for possible inaccuracies in his report: "Of the Communicants above reported, 17, although probably residents of Chapel Hill during the war, are likely to be returned from other Parishes also. Sixteen others, probably not reported elsewhere, can nevertheless scarcely be said to be living here permanently"; *JPEC* 47 (1863), 45.

Table 1. Communicants, Catechumens, and Rectors, 1846–1869[64]

Date	Communicants	Catechumens	Rector Reporting	Families
1846	22w–2c	25		8
1847	22	25w		8
1848	-	15	Olmsted	9
1849	21w–1c		Davis	
1850	29w	38	Davis	9
1851	29		Hubbard	
1852	27	17	Hubbard	
1853	27w	15w	Wheat	
1854	42w–1c	23w	Wheat	
1855	36	20w	Wheat	
1856	37w	60w–20c	Lee	
1857	43w	50w	Lee	
1858	48w	45w	Lee	
1859			Parish vacant (Wheat)	
1860	55w–1c	25	Forbes	
1861	57w–2c	25	Hilliard	
1862	80w–2c	25w–75c	Hilliard	
1863	108w–5c	25w–50c	Hilliard	
1864	87w–5c	20w–30c	Hilliard	
1865			Hilliard resigned, no report	
1866			No report	
1867	"not far from 50"		Hubbard	
1868	38	20	Hubbard	
1869			Parish vacant	

[64] These figures are taken from the yearly reports of the JPEC. The numbers are often broken into "white" (w) or "colored" (c), but not infrequently a simple total is given. The numbers given in the 1863 report were revised downward in the following year's report, retrospectively, to 94w–2c.

However, the newcomers seem not seriously to have altered the pre-war pattern of parish life; earlier features continue to be seen during the war years. Baptisms were still regular occurrences: twenty-two of whites, eighteen of blacks, the latter usually presented by pre-war parishioners: W. P. Mallett (four), Battle (three), C. P. Mallett (three), Mickle (one), Smith (one), with one interesting novelty—the rector himself brought forward two black children for baptism. Marriages were perhaps more frequent in the war than before: four between white couples, one between blacks. And it seems particularly impressive that confirmations were able to continue: Bishop Atkinson visited Chapel Hill four times between 1861 and 1864 to hold confirmation rites, even though the classes were much smaller than they had been in the 1850s, and university students were no longer a presence in them.

Yet there is one striking novelty about the wartime confirmations. Blacks—slaves—had been baptized and married before at the Chapel of the Cross, but in the confirmation rite of 28 March 1863 for the first time two "colored" women were *confirmed* here, Albina Mears and Margaret Smith; both are also separately entered in an 1860 list of communicants updated to 1864, with the later notation "removed" indicating that they had subsequently left the parish. The rite of confirmation is like that of marriage in going far beyond what slave evangelization had envisaged carrying out. I have not been able to identify the former confirmand, but it seems not improbable that she was a servant member of a refugee household that by 1864 had decided that it was worth risking a return to home. As regards a "Margaret Smith," however, it is an excess of information that makes identification difficult. In the communicant list of 1860/4 the name (as "*Mrs.* Margaret Smith") appears immediately after those of Prof. H. Smith and Mrs. H. Smith, raising the possibility that she was a member of their household. Hildreth Hosea Smith (b. 1820) graduated from Bowdoin College in 1842 and took an MA there in 1845; he took up the chair of modern languages at UNC in 1857 and held it until 1868. He became an Episcopalian on his arrival; he and his wife Mary are both on the communicant list of 1858, and he was confirmed here by Bishop Atkinson in October of that year. They took their new church very seriously: their newly-born daughter Lizzie was baptized in the COTC in November 1859, and the son who followed was baptized here in 1864. The Slave Schedule of 1860 reports that by that time Smith had acquired four slaves—a female of 58, a male of 16, a female of 15, and an infant of 1—and our register shows that he presented two of his slaves, Bob and Margaret, for baptism at the COTC in March 1863. The teen-aged Margaret is not likely to have been the "*Mrs.* Margaret Smith" of the communicant list. On the other hand, it is not at all inconceivable that the Smiths had trusted the older female slave on their arrival with the running of their household, had taken an increasing interest in her, and had eventually prepared her for the confirmation recorded in 1863 and her ensuing church membership with us. But other hypotheses are perfectly possible too.

When Bishop Atkinson returned to Chapel Hill for confirmations the next spring (25 April 1864), 5 of his 15 confirmands were again recorded as "colored": David Moore, Cornelius Burnett, Laura Smith, Emma Smith, and Eliza Mallett, all duly recorded as members of the parish ("communicants") on the 1864 list subsequently drawn up by Hilliard—and all of these individuals prove to have been Orange County residents. It will be worth looking more closely at these five. We find in the register that a "Cornelius Burnet" was baptized, admitted to communion, and confirmed in April 1864, all in a matter of three days! The 1860 federal census places a Cornelius Burnett, aged 5, within his father's household in "dwelling 104" of the village enumeration; his father is identified as Charles J. Burnett, aged 44, barber, with an estate valued at $5,000. The father was a figure memorable enough to have found a mention in Kemp Battle's history of the university:

> *I must not omit the restaurant keepers, both of whom were free negroes and of high character. One was Dave Moore, whose business was conducted opposite the Chapel Hill (then Eagle) Hotel. He had relatives in Ohio and sometimes visited them. He was prosperous, and during the war was known in addition to land, to have several hundred dollars in silver concealed. He died suddenly of heart disease. . . . The other caterer to the stomachs of the students was Charles J. Burnett, likewise well-to-do. He and his family emigrated to Ohio and prospered. He gave his children a good education at Oberlin and they became teachers in Graded Schools. Burnett's combined dwelling and restaurant was a few yards East of Moore's.[65]*

It is worth noting, parenthetically, that the Burnett family lived close to (white) communicants of the Chapel of the Cross: Rebecca Lucas and her family were nearby in dwelling 103, F. M. Hubbard in 98, Amanda McDade in 110. (The president of the university, David L. Swain, was enumerated in dwelling 101.) Residential racial segregation was not as universal during slavery as it became later.[66]

Battle's account would suggest that the David Moore ("free colored") who was baptized, admitted to communion, and confirmed together with Cornelius Burnett in 1864, was the colleague of Cornelius's father Charles named by Battle: Moore too is identified in the census as "barber," aged 44, with an estate of $4,400, and his census residence is given as dwelling 108. But this raises a perplexing question. Cornelius Burnett would have been only 9 in 1864, astonishingly young for a confirmand: Robina Mickle, confirmed in the same class, was 16; Kate Fetter, also in that class, was 14. It would seem much more probable that "Cornelius"

---

[65] Battle, *History*, 1:606.

[66] "There was apparently little or no residential segregation in Chapel Hill during slavery. Free black families lived interspersed with white families, and there were even a number of households headed by African Americans that included white household members"; Chapman, "Black Freedom," p. 30.

is in fact a mistake for "Charles," and that the two barber-restaurateurs, friends and neighbors, were being brought into the church and confirmed at the same time, especially since "Cornelius Burnett" is twice referred to in the register as a "free colored *adult*." At the Burnett baptism on 24 April that began the hasty process, Andrew Mickle stood as sponsor; it seems more likely that he would have done this for an adult neighbor (the Mickles were enumerated in dwelling 117) than for a nine-year-old boy; as something of an entrepreneur it is not surprising that Mickle would have been ready to pull strings to bring two influential figures in the free black community into the church quickly, if that was what they wanted—but why should they have wanted it? We simply do not know enough about the dynamics of postwar Chapel Hill society even to guess at motivation.

"David Moore" and "Cornelius Burnett" are the first two names in a list of five under the rubric "colored" that concludes the enumeration of confirmands at Bishop Atkinson's service of 25 April 1864. The other three were not *free* colored residents of the village; they were "servants," slaves serving a household. Two of them, "Laura Smith" and "Emma Smith," are two of Mary Ruffin Smith's four mixed-race nieces, at that moment aged 12 and 18 respectively (they had been baptized ten years before); why her other two nieces (Cornelia and Annette) were not there is impossible to say. Unlike Moore and Burnett, the two girls did not then immediately pass on to the communion table, but it was certainly open to them; Laura first took communion on 3 July of that year, and Emma too was subsequently listed among the parish communicants. Eight months later Emma was married in the Chapel of the Cross to Henry Morphis, one of W. H. Battle's servants. The third individual confirmed on that April occasion, "Eliza Mallett," had her first communion on the following Whitsunday (15 May), and is identified in the register as the "servant" of C. P. Mallett. As far as I can tell, the only enslaved persons who had previously been communicants at COTC were Nanny Green and perhaps "Mrs. Margaret Smith" (above, p. 32).

This is wonderful detail, which leads to innumerable unanswerable questions. Clearly the bishop, the rector (F. M. Hilliard), and the congregation were fully prepared by 1864 to accept some black individuals as communicants, free *or* enslaved, when they presented themselves with the support of members of the congregation. But what the specific dynamics were that led Andrew Mickle to propose Charles Burnett for membership in his congregation, or C. P. Mallett to single out Eliza from his other slaves to the same end, cannot presently be known. Again, all these confirmations came in the last year of the war—there is nothing similar to be found in earlier pages of the register.[67]

---

[67] Malone, *Episcopal church*, 14–15, gives selected statistics from the church in North Carolina as a whole for 1863–64: 401 white baptisms (adults and children), 262 colored; 290 white confirmations, 20 colored. The corresponding numbers for the Chapel of the Cross in these years are: baptisms, 11 white and 13

All this sacramental activity began rapidly to dissipate after the war. It is symptomatic that after the wartime rector abruptly resigned in the late spring of 1865 and returned circuitously to Edenton, leaving his parishioners to conduct what services they could by themselves,[68] entries in the register become hasty and incomplete, often scribbled in pencil, and they come abruptly to an end in 1867–68 when the university began to collapse and the parish could no longer function. The last baptismal entry is, as it happens, for the son of one of Mary Ruffin Smith's nieces, Emma, the one who had been married in the Chapel of the Cross in 1864:

> *Sept. 29th [1867] Samuel infant child (coloured) of Henry and Emma Morfis*
>
> *The Mother and [blank] Sponsors.*

One might wonder whether Mary Ruffin Smith's name had been the one unintentionally omitted.

4. Recovery

The losing of the war had grim economic consequences for all North Carolina towns, but particularly so for Chapel Hill because of its dependence on the university. The university's Confederate bonds had immediately become worthless, and its future income had to come primarily from tuition—but money was terribly scarce, and students were not applying. In March 1868 a group of friends of the university drew up a plan for the reorganization of its curriculum under an elective system with higher admission and graduation standards, in the hope that that would win back public support. However, this project was overtaken by the calling of a state constitutional convention by the army general governing North Carolina by virtue of the Reconstruction legislation of 1867; a new constitution was adopted in April 1868 that among other things made radical changes in the governance of the university, giving the state governor broad powers over it in his capacity as chairman of its board of trustees. When the new board of trustees met in July, the provisional governor of North Carolina, William Holden, forced the resignation of university president David L. Swain and the existing faculty, and announced that the university would be closed in the fall.

In the following January, Holden and the Trustees installed a faculty of five new professors (most with rather limited credentials) and a new president, Solomon Pool, a former UNC tutor

---

colored; confirmations, 14 white and 7 colored. It would be extremely interesting to develop the comparative figures for a similar period in the 1850s.

[68] "1865 Dec. 6th: Mrs Mary Mallett widow of Col. Edward Mallett: in the absence of the minister of the parish the funeral service was read by Judge Battle."

in mathematics.[69] It was generally understood that no one who was not a Republican needed to hope for an appointment; Pool had established his credentials by accusing the school of having hitherto been governed by an aristocracy and family influence and urging that it should be "thoroughly loyalized." (It did not hurt that his brother John was a Republican who represented North Carolina in the US Senate.) Holden talked of instituting a new "people's university," but the General Assembly (though itself overwhelmingly Republican) showed no interest in funding it. Almost no students showed up to attend when it reopened in that spring of 1869, even though Pool had instituted a "Preparatory Department" within the university for school-children aged 12 and above to attend, hoping that would swell its numbers. In spring 1870 there were just 9 University students and 15 Preparatory schoolboys enrolled at Chapel Hill, despite the fact that tuition was now free. One of the original five new professors had left and failed to return, and another did the same that fall; their duties were loaded onto the remaining three. When Holden was impeached in 1870 and removed from office by the General Assembly, there was no longer anyone interested in a "people's university," nor were there funds to support one; only fifteen potential students appeared in the fall of 1870, of whom just two were still present in January 1871. The remnant of the new faculty packed its bags and left; and now the University of North Carolina was definitely closed—though Pool refused to resign and eventually collected his back pay from the years of its closure.

These events had immediate consequences for our parish. The hasty departure of its temporary rector (Hilliard) immediately after the war had meant that once more it could look only to the university for a new one, and Professor Fordyce Hubbard had consented to take up the role again. He filled it from 1866 until 1868, when Governor Holden forced the resignation of the entire faculty; since Hubbard and his family could not live on the meagre rector's salary that was all that was left to them, they left the village and resettled in New York.

---

[69] There is great variance among historians' opinions on the relative roles of Holden and Pool in bringing about the temporary collapse of the University of North Carolina: readers who want a sense of the variance may look at, for example, Horace W. Raper, *William W. Holden: North Carolina's Political Enigma* (Chapel Hill and London: UNC Press, 1985), 121–26; and William D. Snider, *Light on the Hill* (Chapel Hill and London: UNC Press, 1992), chap. 5. There was a similar variance among contemporary observers: Cornelia Phillips Spencer blamed both with equal bitterness, while Kemp Plummer Battle was much harsher on Pool than on Holden. Because my concern in this introduction is with the Chapel of the Cross and its parishioners, and how they perceived their situation, I have chosen to draw my outline of events from Kemp Battle's *History of the University of North Carolina*. He was a participant in some of these events (he and his father William H. were both in the group of friends that worked for a reorganization of the university in 1868, before Holden took the university in a new direction); he was in law practice with his father, who was the most committed churchman in the Chapel of the Cross; and I think it likely that his interpretation of events reflects his father's, which would also have been communicated to the other core members of our parish.

Many other families left Chapel Hill too in these years, thirty at least, moving to new lives elsewhere in North Carolina or in the United States; the village was almost dead. One uncompromising resident who did *not* leave, Cornelia Phillips Spencer (she had married in 1855 and taken her husband's name), wrote in March 1870: "Chapel Hill was never quite so low. You may walk from end to end at eleven o'clock in the day, and not see six people. I am writing letters. It is the only thing I can do."[70] "I am now allowed to go up to the University Library when I please. Books take the place of society."[71] There was nothing to buy and no money to buy it with; one had to raise one's own food somehow, perhaps planting potatoes in the front yard. Farming was difficult: mules and horses had been commandeered when the Union army occupied the village for two weeks in the spring of 1865. Chapel Hillians—those who stayed—were thrown on their own resources, whether black or white; we who have lived through the coronavirus pandemic should have no difficulty in appreciating their day-to-day struggles for economic and psychological survival, which were not unlike ours. The state economy took years to recover, and only in 1875 had things improved enough that the legislature decided it was worthwhile to pay off the university's debts and prepare to open it again.

And how did the parish as a whole bear up under these trying circumstances? At the beginning of the war, in 1861, the Chapel of the Cross had perhaps 35 communicants, of varying degrees of commitment. In 1864 it had considerably more than that, given the influx of refugees. After the war, however, not surprisingly, the parish shrank in tandem with the rest of the village.[72] Cornelia Spencer unintentionally called attention to its losses in writing to a friend in 1869:

> *Some of our citizens are even now on their way to California. Some are in Louisiana. . . . Judge Battle is removing his household goods from his beautiful home—dear to him for 25 years—to begin life afresh. . . . Prof. Martin is in Tennessee. Prof. Hepburn is in Ohio. Dr. Hubbard is in New York. Prof. Smith [he had been a regular communicant since his confirmation in 1858] is in Lincolnton. Prof. Fetter is preparing to move to Henderson.[73]*

---

[70] Letter of March 1870, quoted in Chamberlain, *Old Days*, 184.

[71] Letter of 28 December 1870, quoted in ibid., 193.

[72] The parish did not make a report to the 1866 convention; perhaps Hubbard did not yet feel in command of things after taking over from the departed Hilliard. In 1867, however, Hubbard reported vaguely that "the number of communicants is not far from 50"; *JPEC* 51 (1867), 64. In 1868, on the eve of the university's closure and his departure, he reported that the number was 38; *JPEC* 52 (1868), 102.

[73] Letter to the editor of the *Sentinel*, March 31, 1869; quoted in *Selected Papers of Cornelia Phillips Spencer* [hereafter *SPCPS*], ed. Louis R. Wilson (Chapel Hill: UNC Press, 1953), 662.

Hubbard's departure for New York in the fall of 1868 meant there was no further prospect of a sacramental life there for Episcopalians, for there could be no point in searching for a new rector. The parish had essentially collapsed. When in 1876 the Pittsboro rector explored the prospects for a revived parish in a recovering North Carolina, there were only 24 potential communicants he could still identify in Chapel Hill.

The parish was not totally lacking in spiritual attention during those eight years, to be sure, as fitful evidence shows. Cornelia Spencer wrote in September 1869 that "I went to the Episcopal Church last Sunday and joined them at Communion, having asked permission. . . . About a dozen at Church."[74] Who the celebrant was, she does not say. Bishop Atkinson visited Chapel Hill in June 1871 to preach and confirm; in the same year, probably on the same occasion, Robert Sutton, the rector of St. Bartholomew's, Pittsboro, collected $2.50 from Chapel of the Cross attendees for a diocesan contribution.[75] By 1872 the church fabric seems to have been in obvious decay, for Cornelia Spencer wrote in July: "The Episcopal church gates are nailed up. . . . How changed!"[76] Bishop Theodore Lyman expressed similar dismay after an episcopal visit in June 1874:

> *Since the closing of the University, only occasional services have been held here; the congregation has been greatly diminished, and the means for the support of the Church very considerably decreased. I found the Church edifice sadly in need of repair, and endeavored to have something done, to arrest the progress of decay.*[77]

His endeavors seem to have had no immediate effect.

Figure 7. Robert Sutton. From NCPedia, https://www.ncpedia.org/biography/sutton-robert-bean

But in the improving economic climate of 1875, in the wake of the university's re-opening, a new vestry was organized in October. Our earliest book of vestry minutes opens with an entry stating that

> *at a meeting of the Congregation of the Chapel of the Cross at Chapel Hill on Tuesday, October 26th 1875, . . . to elect a vestry for the Parish for the remainder*

---

[74] Letter of 8 September 1869, quoted in *SPCPS*, 175.

[75] *JPEC* 56 (1872), 23; ibid., 55 (1871), 31.

[76] Article of 10 July 1872, *SPCPS*, 662.

[77] *JPEC* 59 (1875), 38. Lyman had been elected coadjutor bishop in 1873.

of the canonical year, . . . the election was held by ballot, and the result was that more than two thirds of the votes were given for the following gentlemen:

> Messrs. John Kimberly
> Andrew Mickle
> Geo. T. Winston
> Dr. Wm. P. Mallet
> Mr J. DeB. Hooper.[78]

It is not hard to imagine that the outcome had been settled beforehand, for at that moment the "Congregation" of the Chapel of the Cross did not extend much beyond the families of those who were elected.

During the previous eight years the congregation had had no rector, and its very building had been left to decay: might perhaps its vestry have disappeared too? The proceedings of that new vestry of 1875 make no reference to a predecessor, and indeed one member declared that no earlier minutes could be found: writing in 1878, the then Senior Warden went on to say ruefully that "at one time [during those years] there were not a sufficient number of male members to form a vestry."[79] In 1873 the Diocesan Convention actually refused to accept a delegate from the Chapel Hill church because its certificate stated that "a delegate had been appointed without intimating that a vestry had acted or even exists, furthermore it is signed by the Warden, instead of the Secretary of the vestry."[80] On balance, it seems likely that the vestry of 1875 was a new creation, an initiative by a group of Chapel Hill parishioners to resurrect their parish, to bring it back to vitality.[81] If a vestry *had* existed in those difficult

---

[78] Vestry Minutes 1875–1891, p. 3; the actual election took place on 30 October (p. 5); Archives, COTC.

[79] Kemp P. Battle, "Brief History of the Parish . . .," in Register 2, p. 9; Archives, COTC.

[80] *JPEC* 57 (1873), 17.

[81] The account given by Kemp Plummer Battle in 1878 does not contradict that suggestion: "The writer [Battle is writing] of the above has been unable to find the vestry book prior to 1875. Additional facts connected with the history of the parish could doubtless be obtained from it. The officers of the Vestry from 1849 to 1868 were the Hon. William H. Battle, Senior Warden, Andrew Mickle, Junior Warden, Professor [Manuel] Fetter much of that time Secretary. Mr Mickle has been Treasurer since 1849"; Kemp P. Battle, "Brief History," in Register 2, p. 9; Archives, COTC. Manuel Fetter was professor of Greek at UNC 1837–68, was one of the subscribers of the Church of the Atonement in 1842, and figures on its rolls in 1860. But Battle's remarks of 1878 do not encourage the belief that he had any knowledge of a vestry in continuing existence during the years 1868–75, rather the contrary.

There is nothing inconsistent in Battle's statement with the likelihood that a vestry was assembled when Olmsted arrived as rector in 1849 and that it was still in existence when the university first closed in 1868, as two pieces of evidence seem to confirm. The church's earliest register records the

intervening years, it had paid no attention to the steady decline in the church's fabric, while the very first thing the new vestry decided to do after coming into being was to arrange to have the church's roof and guttering repaired, to provide a new tin roof for the tower, to replaster the interior, and to repair the fences around the building.[82] Once that was settled, they arranged for the restoration of regular services, agreeing to ask Robert Sutton to ride up from Pittsboro to Chapel Hill on the second Sunday of every month (a fifteen-mile ride each way) to hold services, promising him $10 on each occasion.[83] Not only did Sutton agree, but the relation developed into something more formal: Sutton reported to the Diocesan convention in June 1877 that he was now "officiating" at the Chapel of the Cross, where he had a congregation of 8 families and 19 communicants.[84] In his history of the parish, Archibald Henderson seems to have had the impression that this relationship had existed ever since 1868,[85] but there is no evidence at all for that: the new vestry had had to start afresh, and to try to bring about a revival from scratch.

What had held the sense of a "Congregation" together in these years, without a priest, with no formal institutional framework, and a decaying physical plant? Fewer than forty communicants in 1861, perhaps twenty a quarter of a century later; what do we know about those who remained committed? All had been members of the much larger pre-war congregations, but while others had left or fallen away after the war ended, three families— those of W. H. Battle, W. P. Mallett, and Andrew Mickle—had persisted in understanding themselves to be members of a continuing community, though their church had closed and

---

funeral in April 1852 of "Mr. Thomas Lloyd Moore, one of the Wardens of this parish," which is certainly an indication that a vestry of some sort was in existence at that time; this must be the T. L. Moore who had been the second person (after J. DeB. Hooper) to sign the document creating the Church of the Atonement in 1842. And when F. M. Hubbard left his post at the Chapel of the Cross in November 1868, "a meeting of the Vestry of the parish of the Chapel of the Cross" drew up a formal testimonial of regret, to be "entered by the Clerk of the Vestry on the records of the Parish." But from that point on there are no similar direct references to a parish vestry, or to its actions, until the new vestry suddenly constituted itself in October 1875.

[82] Vestry Minutes 1875–91, p. 9 (of 12 November 1875); Archives, COTC.

[83] Ibid., pp. 11–12 (of 20 November 1875); Archives, COTC.

[84] JPEC 61 (1877), 182. It was natural for the vestry to think of turning to Sutton. Ever since arriving in Pittsboro in 1860, he had welcomed the opportunity to serve not just his own congregation but other communities all around; in diocesan summaries he reported as rector not only in Pittsboro but in Deep River (St. Mark's) as well, and for a mission church in Haywood, where he held services on the 5th Sunday of the month.

[85] Henderson, Church of the Atonement, 48.

there was no minister. Today's parish has coped with the COVID pandemic largely by the leadership of its staff; but in the post-war "pandemic" of 1868–75 it was necessarily *lay* conviction that held it together: there *was* no staff. Perhaps it is worth noting that those three heads of household had had responsibility engrained into them by their occupations: a lawyer, a physician, and a successful merchant.

What were these few individuals able to do in those eight years, in the absence of a priest and a sacramental life, to maintain their identity as a continuing coherent parish? They could reinforce it by perhaps paying occasional priests to visit, and in their absence by maintaining services led by lay readers commissioned by the bishop—W. H. Battle, Charles P. Mallett, and Andrew Mickle did this in the 1860s.[86] They could continue to scrape together a parochial contribution to diocesan needs to maintain their visibility, and in fact they sent between $10 and $15 (a not inconsiderable sum) virtually every year to the diocesan Episcopal and Contingent fund. They could increase that visibility further by sending delegates to the annual Diocesan Conventions. Even rector-less, they continued to send W. H. Battle as their convention delegate every year from 1869 to 1871, and again in 1873. Though their determination may have been wearing thin—Battle moved his family's church membership to Raleigh in 1874—in the end their efforts were successful. What Sutton discovered in Chapel Hill, after eight years in which Green's chapel had been essentially abandoned, was a tiny, self-conscious, living community that had not lost either its commitment or its identity: a core group persisted, undaunted, that still thought of itself as members of the old Chapel of the Cross.

And as one might expect, it was members of that core group who moved to organize a new vestry in October 1875, as the university came back to life and the local economy revived. Perhaps they were stimulated to do so by an appointment to the revived university, John DeBerniere Hooper (1811–86). Hooper had been one of the original subscribers to the Chapel of the Cross (as the "Church of the Atonement") in 1842, and his first child was baptized by W. M. Green in 1839 (Green baptized a second in 1848). Hooper had graduated from UNC in 1831 and had soon been appointed professor of modern languages and of Latin there, but left in 1848 to teach in private schools.[87] He was now returning to Chapel Hill as professor of Greek and French, together with his wife Mary Elizabeth and their daughter Julia; might not the moment have seemed opportune to core members Andrew Mickle and William P. Mallett to re-establish an Episcopal vestry? As we have seen, the new entity at first comprised Mickle, Mallett, and Hooper, as well as a fourth man, John Kimberly, who had been professor of agricultural chemistry 1861–66 and had returned to that position in 1875. When Kimberly

---

[86] Battle, "Brief History," pp. 8–9.

[87] A portrait of Hooper as professor is in Battle, *History*, 1:545–46.

decided to leave the university in 1876 (after his wife's death that year), another old-core family member took his place on the vestry and became its Senior Warden—W. H. Battle's son Kemp, who had just (June 1876) become president of the revived University. We have met him as well.

All these men had known one other for a long time, and had shared a great deal. Three of the four had known W. M. Green personally from thirty years before, and had memories of the Chapel of the Cross when it was still the Church of the Atonement; they all had personal as well as professional attachments to the old university, and could remember the early days when liturgically-minded Episcopalians stood out somewhat defensively in a nominally Presbyterian community. It would not be unreasonable, I think, to suppose that these men had decided that this was the right moment to formally institutionalize their collective commitment to a revived Chapel of the Cross. In order to make up the necessary numbers for a vestry, they drafted the young George Winston (he had been a sophomore when the university began its collapse in 1868, and had just been appointed professor of Latin and German; he was not an Episcopalian) to be their Secretary. They could scarcely have imagined that Winston, like Battle, would go on to become president of the University.[88]

One other person would be essential to the eventual resurrection of the parish—especially after her death.[89] Mary Ruffin Smith had been fully occupied in directing the affairs of the Chatham County plantation during the war and then afterwards, when the parish had disintegrated—her brothers were unfit to do so.[90] Her one continuing contact with the old parish community seems to have been her close friendship with William Horn Battle, and one might guess that it was Battle who informed her that the parish was being constituted anew: when its first list of communicants was drawn up, on 13 May 1876, the first name set down was "Miss Mary R. Smith." Judge Battle himself moved his church membership back from Raleigh to Chapel Hill in January 1877, no doubt with great satisfaction.

---

[88] Once the parish numbers seemed to have stabilized, on 2 April 1877, Winston resigned his position on the vestry, saying "The fact that my continuing a vestryman is no longer necessary to a full organization of the Vestry and the belief that one who is not a member of the church should not under ordinary circumstances be a member of the Vestry have induced me to take this step"; Vestry minutes 1875–91, p. 27; Archives, COTC. Only a few years later, however, when the leaders of the congregation had begun to die and the congregation was again greatly reduced in numbers, Winston overcame his scruples and accepted re-election to the vestry; Ibid., p. 133, entry for 6 September 1885.

[89] The COTC was one of the chief beneficiaries of the complicated settlement of Mary Ruffin Smith's estate after she died in 1885; Jones, *Miss Mary's Money*, chaps. 6–7, 9.

[90] Ibid., p. 110; on the gradual decay of her brothers, see chaps. 3 and 4.

The new vestry cannot have helped realizing that the parish could not be reborn without money. Much of their first year was occupied with assessing what needed to be done to bring the abandoned building back into usable condition; then they turned to the problem of securing a rector again. Their arrangement with Robert Sutton had been valuable, but they needed a permanent solution. Before the war, the few Chapel Hill parishioners had never been able to raise money enough to support a rector satisfactorily; post-war, the vestry guessed that an annual salary of $500 might be required to attract one. In 1878 they asked for pledges from parishioners for that specific purpose, with a result that suggested that that sum might be within their reach:[91]

William Horn Battle	*$80*
Kemp P. Battle	*$120*
W. P. Mallett	*$50*
George T. Winston	*$15*
J. DeB. Hooper	*$50*
A. Mickle and Son	*$25*
F. M. Simonds	*$12*
Mrs. S[usan] M. Barbee	*$10*
Mrs. Sarah A. Taylor	*$30*
R. H. Graves	*$15*
Miss Mary R. Smith	*$50*
Miss Maria Spear	*$6*

Again, most of these names are familiar to us from the pre-war parish, and many of the unfamiliar ones turn out to reveal that the parish would once again have to depend almost entirely on its appeal to the university faculty to ensure its existence: as we have seen, George Winston was its new professor of classical languages, elected by a fresh Board of Trustees in 1875 (which elected Andrew Mickle as university bursar on the same occasion); F. M. Simonds was UNC's new professor of geology (unfortunately he developed acute pneumonia in 1878 and had to move to California); and Robert Graves was its professor of engineering and also, probably not irrelevantly, the son-in-law of J. DeB. Hooper (he had married Julia Hooper in 1877).[92] The vestry must have recognized that they had serious problems ahead of them.

As it proved, their initiative was successful almost immediately. After a year under Robert Sutton, "priest-in-charge," the parish was able to call a new rector, Joseph Blount Cheshire,

---

[91] Vestry minutes 1875–91, pp. 35–36 (of 25 March 1878); Archives, COTC.

[92] Thumbnail sketches are supplied in Battle, *History*, 2: 80–83, where Battle gives an unusually warm personal appreciation of Andrew Mickle.

Jr., who had been ordained deacon on Easter 1878 and began his parochial duties in Chapel Hill four weeks later, initially under Sutton's guidance. One of the first things he did was to list his parishioners in the church register, 43 of them: they included the familiar names, Battles and Saunders and Malletts and Mickles and Hoopers, but also fourteen "students in the university"; the parish was evidently once again becoming a home for Episcopalians at UNC. Most of those students had left by end of the next academic year, but they were replaced by another fourteen in 1879–80.

Cheshire must have been a dynamic presence, full of energy. His entries in the register are much more careful and more detailed than his predecessors', and from the beginning of his tenure he kept close records of the parochial finances. He established a Mission Station in Durham (St. Philip's), and often went to that city to officiate at funerals, to conduct baptisms in private homes, and once to celebrate a wedding (in the Methodist church). It is perhaps no wonder that he did not remain in a small backwater. In 1880 Cheshire was ordained priest and was formally made rector of the Chapel of the Cross, but the next year he was called to become rector at St. Peter's, Charlotte, one of the largest parishes in the diocese. During the next twelve years he proved an active and effective figure not only in that parish but in the wider diocese, and when Bishop Lyman asked for an assistant bishop, Cheshire was elected in October 1893. Two months later, on Bishop Lyman's death, he became diocesan.

Figure 8. Joseph Blount Cheshire Jr. From William Stevens Perry, *The Bishops of the American Church, Past and Present.* (New York: The Christian Literature Co, 1897).

Cheshire's formal entries in the register end on p. 102, and are followed by nine blank pages. They signal the end of an era in our church's history. All the people who had shaped and maintained the parish from its earliest days through the Civil War, and remained faithful to it during its hiatus after the war, died in the 1880s: Judge Battle (actually in 1879), Laura Saunders in 1881, Mary Ruffin Smith in 1885, Andrew Mickle in 1886, William P. Mallett in 1889. John DeB. Hooper, the parish's last direct link to its 1842 foundation, died in 1886. Its next era would confront the same problems of leadership (after Cheshire, five rectors were called in the 1880s, each quickly resigning) and financing. That is a different story, however, a future history that will have to be told from other sources. Even so, there are occasional hints in our register that already let us look a little way into the future legacy of the early COTC.

5. In Search of Motivation

It is an inescapable consequence of data collections like our first parish register that they tell us what happened but not why. The motives of the individuals involved in events, their intentions, their beliefs and convictions, are not part of the record. We have been repeatedly brought up against this limitation here. Why did Andrew Mickle have some of his slaves baptized but not all? More broadly, did individual members of our parish espouse slave evangelization (as they certainly did) out of Christian conviction, or a desire to control? Can we assume that the attitudes towards slavery, individual and collective, of recent Northern academic immigrants to the south were bound to be the same as those of Southerners who had grown up with the system for generations? Without outside sources of information, it is almost impossible to understand the deeper meaning of particular events. If only we had had a gossipy Cornelia Phillips among the parishioners of the Chapel of the Cross! But if we did, her letters have still to be found.

Yet in exceptional cases a sequence of events goes so far beyond coincidence that it forces a sense of intentionality upon us. As we have seen, parishioners at the antebellum COTC frequently presented their slaves for baptism, sometimes as infants, sometimes as adults. When their slaves were married in a religious ceremony, as sometimes also happened, the owners' permission for the wedding was a prerequisite. (The marriages had no legal status, however, since before the Civil War North Carolina law precluded slaves from entering into contracts, including marriage.)[93] One cannot help but wonder whether the impulse for such ceremonies came from the master, moved perhaps by a vague impulse towards slave evangelization (though Graebner does not suggest that slave marriages were encouraged by the same ideal as were baptisms), or from the slave, out of catechesis and a developing religious sense, perhaps, or simply to win the approval of a devout master. Ordinarily this question of agency has to remain a matter of speculation for lack of evidence, as in so many other cases, but in one instance our parish register furnishes considerable evidence to fuel our speculations.

Judge William Horn Battle joined his wife Lucy's Episcopal denomination in 1843 and committed fully to his wife's creed for the rest of his life, as we have seen. In 1844 the couple had four of their children baptized in the Chapel of the Cross; two more soon followed the same path. The Battles showed no particular interest in slave evangelization, however, and did not present any of their many slaves for baptism upon joining. Instead, and quite remarkably, in the first few years after joining the Chapel of the Cross the Battles arranged for the *marriage* there of three of their female slaves: Lizzie to Sam (Morphis) in 1845,[94] Jane to Washington

---

[93] Johnson, *Ante-bellum North Carolina*, 536–37.

[94] Kemp Battle (*History*, 1:202) writes: "Sam Morphis was a picturesque mulatto, a slave, but allowed to 'hire his own time,' i. e., to regulate his own actions on paying his master, James M. Morphis, who

(Snipes) in 1847,[95] and Judy to Tom (Kirby) in 1848[96]—William Mercer Green performed all three ceremonies. Still more remarkably, at a service on Easter Day in 1856 the children who had been born to these three marriages were baptized at a collective ceremony at the Chapel of the Cross—five Morphis children, three daughters born to Jane <Snipes>, now widowed, and a Kirby son—with W. H. Battle's wife Lucy and their daughter Susan standing as sponsors to all six!

Surely it is not over-speculative to look for meaning here, to suppose that for some reason the Battles had kept an approving eye on these particular slave pairings from their very inception and had now arranged for a festal concelebration of the slave children's baptisms, no doubt assuming the agreement of the parents. We might even go further and suppose that the three women involved were all domestic servants of whom Lucy Battle had thought particularly well, since she and her daughter made a point of being the family presence in the

---

removed from this state to Texas, author of a history of that state, a stipulated sum per annum. This was against the law, but that was evaded by his having a white man, John H. Watson, to be his nominal hirer. Sam was very handsome, full of humor, an expert manager of horses. His occupation was to drive hacks (as the passenger carriages in use were called), a lucrative business before the advent of railroads." His recollections of his life were collected about 1896 and are recorded in http://freepages.rootsweb.com/~orangecountync/history/peeps/Morphis/Morphis.html. His chronology is not entirely trustworthy, but his account of his marriage is interesting: "I was married by the Rev. Professor [William Mercer Green], afterwards Bishop of Mississippi. My wife was a 'house-girl' in the home of the Professor of Law, Judge B[attle]. We were married on the porch of Judge B[attle]'s house. A large number of students came to witness the ceremony." See further Kim Smith, "Book of Harriet: The Disambiguation of Five North Carolinian Siblings 1840–1941" (Master's Project, Master of Arts in Liberal Studies, Duke University, 2016), 86–90.

[95] Battle, *Memories*, 246, describes the wedding of the daughter of Jinny, the Battle family cook, "with the Episcopal service by Rev. William M. Green at the request of the white family. The parties were carefully coached before hand . . . ," and goes on to report that the (unnamed) groom was afterwards murdered near the Battle front gate. Since our register records just three marriages celebrated by Green involving a Battle slave—Sam Morphis to Lizzy Battle in 1845, Washington Snipes to Jane Battle in 1847, and Tom Kirby to Judy Battle in 1848—and since two of these grooms, Morphis and Kirby, were still alive long after the Civil War, it seems probable that Washington Snipes was the murdered groom.

[96] Evidence suggests that Tom Kirby was enslaved at the time of his marriage but was emancipated between 1860 and 1865; he was an assistant janitor in Old West building, and was rumored to make further money by selling whiskey to students (Battle, *History*, 2:560). In Reconstruction Kirby was briefly a member of the Chapel Hill Board of Commissioners. He and Judy had their marriage recertified after the war (since slave marriages had no legal status) on 11 June 1866; Orange County Cohabitation Bonds and Records, 1866–68, p. 179. (I am indebted to Mark Chilton for this reference.) See further Mark Chilton, "Wandering through the NC Piedmont" [blog], March 28, 2009); and Smith, "Book of Harriet," 106–9.

baptismal service.[97] It was a private arrangement, however, extra-parochial; the Kirbys and the Morphises were not members of the congregation (neither was the widowed Jane), and are never listed among the communicants of the parish in the rectors' annual reports. To confirm that a personal relationship was at the origin of these events we can further point out that the Kirby son was baptized "Edward *Plummer*." It is unusual in our register to find two names given to a slave child in baptism, and this instance all the more remarkable when we realize that "Plummer" was Lucy Battle's maiden name! The name would certainly not have been given without her initiative or at least willing consent, and seems to establish that she and her husband had been looking out personally for these particular slaves over the years.

The third of the five Morphis children who were baptized on that Easter Day in 1856, Henry, reappears in our register eight years later. Since his mother was a Battle slave, he had grown up in the Battle household, and on 22 December 1864 we find the marriage recorded between "Henry servant of W. H. Battle & Emma servant of Mary Smith," performed by the rector, Francis Hilliard. Emma was the second oldest of Mary Ruffin Smith's four enslaved nieces, and Mary Smith was quite as dedicated to the Episcopal church as were the Battles, "as strictly High Church as one could be without being a ritualist"; this was no doubt one of the factors in their close friendship: "[as long as] Judge Battle and his family were residents of Chapel Hill," Cornelia Spencer noted, "her association was chiefly with them."[98] Smith and the Battles together might well have promoted the marriage, but in any case they would certainly have been delighted to see two children they had long cared for independently now united at their Chapel of the Cross. They would have been further delighted when Sam, the first child of Henry and Emma, was baptized there on 29 September 1867. Perhaps the Battles arranged for it specially; it was the very last baptism entered in the register before the church was effectively shuttered for the next eight years. Nevertheless, in March 1868 there was another Chapel Hill marriage of relevance to our history, when Edward Plummer Kirby was married to Annette Smith, the third of Mary Smith's nieces, at the Presbyterian church by Charles Phillips.[99] In the light of what we have just learned, it is impossible not to suspect that this was another marriage that was welcomed if not arranged by the Battles and Mary Smith to

---

[97] And her interest in their children could have been reinforced by having often helped bring them into the world. She supervised the births of slave babies, writing in the case of her servant Lizzy (Morphis), whose son—quite possibly Henry—she helped deliver in November 1845: "I assure you I was much relieved as she had a long hard time of it. I sympathized with her a good deal . . ."; W. Conard Gass, "A Felicitous Life: Lucy Martin Battle, 1805–1874," *The North Carolina Historical Review,* 52 (1975), 375–77, where her general concern for her slaves' well-being is emphasized.

[98] Jones, *Miss Mary's Money*, 108–9, quoting Cornelia Phillips Spencer, "A Notable Woman North Carolina Has Produced," *State Chronicle* (Raleigh), February 28, 1886, p. 1; reprinted in *SPCPS*, 710–14.

[99] Jones, *Miss Mary's Money,* 112.

bring together two more young people whose lives they had long followed with affection; the parallel between the Morphis-Smith and the Kirby-Smith marriages is surely too close to be a coincidence. The one disappointment that the white patrons must have felt would have been that there was no longer an Episcopal institution in Chapel Hill where the occasion could take place.

It took only eighteen months more for Mary Ruffin Smith to approve of husbands for her two other nieces: on 14 October 1868 Laura married a Charlotte barber, Grey Toole (who served only white clients), and moved back to Charlotte with him, while on 8 August 1869 Cornelia, the oldest, married Robert Fitzgerald, a Civil War soldier and teacher, born in Delaware, whose family was free before the war—the latter couple were the grandparents of Pauli Murray. There is no hint of a Battle (or COTC) connection in either case (though Laura's wedding was performed by the same minister who had celebrated Annette's marriage seven months before, Charles Phillips).[100]

All this suggests motivation, that some parishioners of the antebellum COTC believed so strongly in the importance of the Episcopal sacraments that they arranged that a few slaves for whom they had come particularly to care might follow a kind of sacramental path as they grew to adulthood, from baptism to marriage, quite different from "slave evangelization." Could their vision of that path have extended to preparing those slaves, as children, for eventual confirmation and communion, so long as they were amenable and receptive to the catechistic instruction that was involved? After all, we know that the parish's pre-war Sunday school included both white and black scholars, that published catechisms both written and oral were an object of study there, and that Lucy Battle herself volunteered to teach in that school.[101] Pauli Murray heard from her grandmother Cornelia that the Smith sisters' aunt Mary "elected to send them to the Chapel of the Cross on the University campus in Chapel Hill *to be trained in the Episcopal faith* [my italics]," and reported that Cornelia "had memorized the Lord's Prayer, Creed, Ten Commandments and Cathechism [*sic*] found in the Book of Common Prayer"[102]—might that have been a feature of that antebellum Sunday School,

---

[100] Pauli Murray's vivid account of her family's history, *Proud Shoes* (New York: Harper, 1956), based on conversations with her grandparents, has much more to say about the Fitzgerald than the Smith side of her lineage, and says nothing about the contrasting circumstances of these four marriages coming so close together (p. 165). She speaks in detail only of her grandparents' match, implying that Mary Ruffin Smith encouraged it from the outset because she knew that Cornelia thought well of the young man, and had then had "the first refreshing conversation she had had in years" when they first talked (217–18). Jones (*Miss Mary's Money*, 112) gives an equally brief summary of the four marriages and also fails to comment on the Battle-Smith connection in the first two.

[101] Gass, "A Felicitous Life," 391.

[102] Murray, *Proud Shoes*, 53, 159.

perhaps? But we are once again speculating beyond our evidence. It is a pity that our register does not give us Sunday school attendance lists, but we must be grateful for all that it <u>does</u> give us!

Still, we have little difficulty in recognizing the persistent influence of the old COTC here and there on these later generations, and not just from our first parish register but from other sources as well. We have seen that Emma and Henry Morphis had their son Sam baptized in 1867 just before the church was temporarily closed. But we happen to know too that when Bishop Lyman paid an episcopal visit to the decaying structure in 1874—a visit omitted from our register—Emma and Henry seized the opportunity to bring their new daughters to be baptized here as well.[103] Cornelia Fitzgerald made sure that her first child, Mary Pauline (b. 1870), was baptized in an Episcopal ceremony, though it had to be in Hillsborough since the COTC was not in use.[104] The register records that by 1880 Cornelia had become a communicant of St. Philip's Mission Station in Durham[105]—St. Philip's was served by our own rector at the time, Joseph Cheshire, and he kept its records with ours. And of course the book *Proud Shoes* is an overriding witness to Cornelia's strong influence on its author, her granddaughter Pauli Murray. It was not by chance that Pauli was ordained as an *Episcopal* priest.

One final COTC marriage of a black couple in these post-war years deserves comment: on 27 September 1866, Susan Kirby was married to Wilson Caldwell by Fordyce Hubbard.

---

[103] Jones, *Miss Mary's Money*, 126, summarizing a letter of Maria Spear dated 9 July 1874 that describes their recent baptism by Bishop Lyman and his confirmation of four other individuals. Lyman recorded the event for the diocesan report as follows: "Second Sunday after Trinity, June 14th [1874], in the Chapel of the Cross, Chapel Hill, after morning prayer by Rev. Mr. Curtis [rector at Hillsborough], preached and administered the Holy Communion, and afterwards administered to a sick person. In the evening Mr. Curtis having been called back to Hillsboro, I read the service, baptized three infants, confirmed four persons and made an address"; *JPEC* 59 (1875), 38. There is no record of these sacraments in our register—not surprisingly, given that there was still no rector in June 1874, and hence no one with the responsibility for keeping a canonical record. The absence of such a record may have helped mislead Jones into his apparent assumption that the bishop involved must have been Thomas Atkinson.

[104] Murray, *Proud Shoes*, 229.

[105] It is quite curious that while Emma and Laura Smith are recorded as confirmed communicants of the COTC (April 1864), their sisters Cornelia and Annette are not. Pauli Murray declared very specifically in *Proud Shoes* that "Grandmother [Cornelia] said that when she was twelve years old [1856; she was born in February 1844 and had been baptized in December 1854] she was confirmed at the chapel along with the daughter of ex-Governor David L. Swain, who was then president of the University" (53), but there is no record at all of such an event in our register. Nor does it seem to have been omitted accidentally; Bishop Atkinson's annual reports to the diocesan convention 1855–60 cite only five occasions on which he confirmed at Chapel Hill, each of which is recorded accurately in our register.

Neither party had had any previous recorded sacramental association with our church, but Susan was the niece of Tom Kirby and Judy Battle, who had been married there in 1848 when enslaved and had had their marriage formally recertified just three months before (above, n. 96); perhaps the event suggested a precedent to their niece. The groom's father, "Doctor November," had been a slave of university president David Swain with the responsibility for serving Old East and South Building, and over time became much respected by faculty and students. His son Wilson (b. 1841) began to serve the University too from his early years, first as a gardener, then as a waiter on the new scientific laboratories, and he was part of the tiny party that went out in April 1865 to meet the Union forces approaching Chapel Hill and to ask that the campus be respected—the group also included William H. Battle, Manuel Fetter, and Andrew Mickle, as well as President Swain, so Wilson Caldwell was a known quantity to at least some COTC parishioners when he was married there the next year.

Figure 9. Wilson Caldwell. From North Carolina Collection, Wilson Library, University of North Carolina.

Caldwell quit his job in disgust in 1868 when the new university administration cut the salaries of employees and faculty, but he returned when the university was reopened on new terms in 1875 and became head of its labor force for many years; even more perhaps than his father he was respected and indeed admired: he held two public offices—Justice of the Peace for a year, and later a member of the Board of Commissioners. He died in 1898, and is buried (like Dilsey Craig, Cornelia Spencer's "Aunt Dilsey") in the old Chapel Hill Cemetery. In the brief account of Caldwell's life drawn up by Kemp Battle three years earlier, celebrating "his uncommon good sense and tact and the propriety of his conduct," Battle mentioned that Caldwell was a member of Chapel Hill's Congregational Church.[106] As our register has repeatedly revealed, the early Chapel of the Cross evidently touched the lives of far more Chapel Hillians, black and white, than its mere communicants.

*   *   *

The preceding survey of the early years of the COTC, built so narrowly around what its first register has to tell us about its institutional and sacramental life, can give only a limited and no doubt distorted account of its broader history. The parish communicants remain little more than names whose lives and thought have to be inferred and reconstructed from public documents: with rare exceptions—Mary Ruffin Smith, the Battle family—they never speak for themselves about their life in the church. And the situation is far worse for those black Chapel Hillians, free and enslaved, who may have been linked to the church in one way or another: Sam Morphis and Wilson Caldwell have both kept some voice, Cornelia Smith's

---

[106] Kemp P. Battle, *Sketch of the Life and Character of Wilson Caldwell* (Chapel Hill: University Press Company, 1895), 8.

memories have been resurrected by her grand-daughter, but most are not even known to us as named individuals. Thus an integral part of the parish community is inevitably hidden from this history, and we must ultimately acknowledge that the picture given here is bound to be to some extent incomplete, and perhaps misleading as well.

We, the subscribers do hereby agree to form ourselves into a Church or Congregation of christian people to be known by the name of the Church of the Atonement, Chapel Hill N. Ca and do also hereby consent to adopt and be governed by the Constitution and Canons of the Protestant Episcopal Church in these United States.

May 13. 1842.

The First Parish Register (1842–1881)
of the Chapel of the Cross

A. M. Hooper

T. L. Moore

S. Robertt

M. Fetter

J. D. B. Hooper

W. S. Green

Jno. M. Craig

Robt. T. Hall

W. M. Green Jr

Geo. Moore

W. D. Jones

J. S. Green

Charlotte Hooper

Mary F. Waddell

Anne C. Hall

Mary C. Hooper

Matilda A. Williams

Sally P. Williams

Mary W. Green

Mary W. Hall

Elizabeth Craig by J. M. Craig

Catharine J. Waddell

Charlotte J. Green

Mrs Jones

THE TEXT OF THE FIRST PARISH REGISTER (1842–1881) OF THE CHAPEL OF THE CROSS, CHAPEL HILL

What follows is a careful transcription, page by page, of the contents of a loosely bound volume now in the archives of the Chapel of the Cross and containing individual entries recording its sacramental activities (and some other business matters) during the years 1842-1881. The volume has eleven un-numbered pages at the beginning, which are here called pages a-k. There follow 115 consecutively numbered pages, and then four more un-numbered pages, here called pages 116-119. ("Pages" is here used loosely, to refer to any blank surface containing writing, for "page a" and "page 119" are used here to denote the blank sides of the front and back boards of the book, both of which contain church records.) At some point in the twentieth century, other early documents have been tipped into the volume, and these are commented on in their proper place.

The entries have been made in different hands, virtually all of which can be identified with one or another of the ten men who served as rector of the parish during those four decades.[1] They do not follow a rigorously consistent format. Some were made with care, some in haste; some were made at time of an event, others well after the fact. Some were written sequentially, others were squeezed in out of chronological order; some are written in ink, others in pencil. This irregularity gives the register a certain charm, revealing it as a living record of the church's life in the middle of the nineteenth century, and rather than cosmetize it by formalizing its entries according to a common standard, I have chosen to reproduce its changing layout and its variable script with some care, helped by a few conventions. I have used black Garamond type to represent writing in ink, italics to indicate pencil. When (as often happened) a rector came back to an entry and emended or corrected it, I have used slashes, /thus/, to identify a later addition. Only occasionally have I felt it necessary to make an editorial comment or

---

[1] Those who may some day have occasion to consult the original document may find it useful to have this record of sample pages where the handwriting of a particular rector can be identified with certainty: William Mercer Green 1842 (1841)-1849: pages a, 119; Aaron F. Olmsted 1848: none found; Thomas F. Davis, Jr. (deacon), 1849-March 1851: pages 4-5; Fordyce M. Hubbard 1851-53, 1865-68: pages 5 (bottom), 6 (top), 16 (bottom), 33 (middle); John Thomas Wheat 1853-56, 1858-60: pp. 6-7; Henry T. Lee 1856-58: pp. 9, 115; E. M. Forbes 1860-61: pp. 12 (top), 116 (bottom); Francis W. Hilliard 1861-65: p. 33 (top); R. B. Sutton (priest-in-charge) 1876-78): p. 33 (bottom), 37; Joseph Blount Cheshire, Jr. (deacon) 1878-1881: p. 62. Some examples can be seen on pages reproduced in this volume. On p. 59, the entries were all made by William Mercer Green. On p. 85, the successive hands are those of Lee, Wheat, Forbes, and Hubbard; on p. 91, those of Hilliard and Hubbard.

clarification, and these are always placed in square brackets. Parentheses and underlines are as present in the register. Complete faithfulness to the original is of course impossible, as can be seen from sample pages, but I hope that the inaccuracies that remain will not impair the usefulness, and vividness, of the text.

_____(p. a = inside of front board) _____

M—   *Feb 26 /1849/*   *A M. L. H & M. H. M. communed*
       March 2nd   *Joseph, infant son of T. W Carr*
                   baptized by W. M. G. privately (in extremis)
                   born Oct. 23^d 1842 died March 9th, 43
                   W. Green Carr, oldest child of above born
                   Oct 13, 1842

       April Easter   *Mary Hall & Mary ..... communed*
March 2nd 1844
         Buried William Jolly
April 22^d 1846   *George F. Mitchell died—buried next day*
                at Hillsborough

_____(pp. b-e blank)_____

_____(p. f) _____

[The following document has been tipped in]

We, the subscribers do hereby agree to form ourselves into a Church or Congregation of christian people to be known by the name of the Church of the Atonement, Chapel Hill N. Ca. and do also hereby consent to adopt and be governed by the Constitution and Canons of the Protestant Episcopal Church in these United States, May 13. 1842.

A. M. Hooper	Charlotte Hooper
T L Moore	Mary F Waddell
J J Roberts	Anne C Hall
M. Fetter	Mary E Hooper
J. D. B. Hooper	Matilda A Williams
S. S. Green	Sally P. Williams
Jno. M. Craig	Mary W. Green
Robt. T. Hall	Mary W. Hall
W. M. Green Jr.	Elizabeth Craig by J. M. Craig
Geo. Moore	Catharine Waddell
J B Jones	Charlotte J. Green
J S Green	Mrs. Jones

_____(p. g) _____

The Parish retained the name written on the other side, till the Consecration of the Church in the fall of 1848, when the name adopted was the Parish of the Chapel of the Cross.

_____(p. h) _____

List of Books purchased for Sunday School of Chapel of the Cross:

1856

Apr. 1 Bill of Books of T. W. Stanford N. York, to wit:

2 Doz. Testaments: 2 sizes:	$2.75	
2 do. Catechisms: No. 2	.48	
2 do. do. Simplified	.75	
2 do. S. S. Book No. 1	.30	
1 do. Oral catechism	.75	
2 Packard's questions	.25	
1 doz. S.S. Liturgy Hymns	1.50	
1 do. Bearen's Help to Cat.ˢ	.85	
½ do. Questions on Acts	.37	
½ do. S. S. Class Books	.30	
2 doz. Tract Primers	3.60	
50 Library Books	8.00	
	$19.90	
Boy trainer for clergyman	.35	
Evidences of Christianity	.45	
Religion as Seen through the Ch	.30	
Little Episcopalian	.35	
	$21.35	
½ Freight on do.	3.25	
	$24.60	

Apr. 25 Bill of books of W. L. Pomeroy

½ doz. S. S. Liturgy	.38
¼ do. do.	.19
1 Copy Help to Catechising	.09
Amt. carried up	$25.26

Apr. 25 Amt. brot. up $25.26

Timid Lucy	.38
Love's Lesson	.38
11 Tract Primers	1.65
1 Tales about the Heathen	.25
1 Trees, Fruits and Flowers	.20
2 "Legion"	.40
1 Keith on Prophecy	.15
1 Scripture Lessons	.15
1 Faith Explained	.15
1 Repentance do.	.15
1 Great Truths	.15
1 Rolls Plumbe	.10
1 Wishing Cap	.15
Tracts 8 Packages	2.05
Helen Morton's Trial	.63
Lamp & Lantern	.40
Last Leaf from S. Side	.50
Happy home	.50
Harry & Archie	.20
Little E [—erased?]	
Amt. forward	$33.80

_____(p. i) _____

1856 Amt. brought forward	$33.80	[on the right, sums in pencil]
Aug. Amt. by Mr. Mickle	5.00	
	$38.80	$38.80

Sep. 21. Books from W.L. P.

2 doz. Tract. Primer	3.60		1.80	
½ do. Scripture Lessons.	.90		.45	
1 do. Union Spel. Book	.75		.37 ½	
[Sep] 29 1 do. do. do.	.75		.37 ½	
2 do. Union primer	.48		.24	
2 do. 1st Reader	.72	1/2	.36	= $6.75
2 do. 2^{d} do.	1.20		.60	
Oct. 9 ½ do. Scripture Less.	.90		.45	
1 do. Great Truths	1.80		.90	
½ do. Scrip. Animals	1.20		.60	
½ do. Trees Fruits etc.	1.20		.60	

1857

Jan. 8 8 packages Embossed gilt Cards 2.00		2.00	
		$47.55	
other ½ of above bill		6.75	
Amt. Total		$54.30	

Amts Charged:

1856. April 1. Bill of T. N. S. as above	$19.90	
½ Freight on Same	3.25	
Oct. 1. Amt. Charged	10.00	
1857 Mar. 6 do. do.	14.40	
	$47.55	
Charged Sep. 7	6.75	
Amt. Total	$54.30	

_____(pp. j-k blank) _____

Baptisms

Berkeley, son of { W. M. Green / Charlotte J. Green } baptized in Raleigh by Bishop
    Ives — Parents & Rev R. S. Mason Sponsors

George Hooper, son of the same, baptized at Chapel Hill Sept 4th 1842 by Rev.
    Thos. F. Davis — Parents & Mrs Charlotte Hooper Sponsors

Duncan Cameron, son of the same baptized at Chapel Hill Dec 8th 184_
    by Rev. W. M. Green,

Helen De Berniere, { J. D. B. Hooper / + / Mary Hooper } baptized by Rev W. M. Green
    May 19th 1839 — Parents & Mrs S Cobia Sponsors

Frances, daughter of the same — baptized Sept. 4th 1842.

Sophia Eliza, wife of Archibald Davis, June 19th 1841

James Francis)
John Wesley { sons of { John Macon Craig) / Elizabeth Craig } May 30th 1841
Mr Harrison)

John Macon Craig)
Elizabeth Craig } adults, June 22nd 1841

Joseph, infant son of J. W. Carr baptized March 1845

_____(p.1) _____

Baptisms

Berkeley, son of W. M. Green & Charlotte J. Green, baptized in Raleigh by Bishop Ives—
    Parents & Rev. R. S. Mason Sponsors

George Hooper, son of the same, baptized at Chapel Hill /Sept. /4th/ 1842/ by
    Rev. Thomas F. Davis. Parents & Mrs. Charlotte Hooper Sponsors.

Duncan Cameron, son of the same baptized at Chapel Hill Dec. 8th 1844
    by Rev. W. M. Green

Helen De Berniere, [daughter of] J. D. B. Hooper & Mary Hooper, baptized by
    Rev. W. M. Green May 19th 1839—Parents & Mrs. L. Cobia Sponsors

Frances, daughter of the same – baptized Sept. 4th 1842

Anne Caroline Swain
David Lowry Swain   ⎦ children of David L. & Eleanor baptized Oct 12th 1840 by W. M. G.
Richd Caswell Swain

Sophia Eliza, wife of Archibald Davis, June 19th 1841

James Francis
John Wesley   ⎦ sons of John Macon Craig & Elizabeth Craig May 30th 1841
Wm Harrison

John Macon Craig
Elizabeth Craig   ⎦ adults, June 22nd 1841

Joseph, infant Son of T.W. Carr, baptized March 1843

_____(p. 2) _____

Baptisms (continued)

Richard Henry
Junius Cullen   ⎦ children of Wm H. & Lucy Battle August 4th 1844
Mary Johns/t/on   Parents & Laura Battle Sponsors
Wesley Lewis

Patrick & Nancy   Children of David and [blank] Caudle, August 4, 1844

Mary Ann Caudle, child of William & [blank]   August 4, 1844

Thomas Stewart Armistead (infant son of Dr Robert Armistead of Plymouth NC)
        baptized by Rev W. M. Green Sept 29th 1844—
        Mrs. Jane Ward & Mrs. Henrietta Jones Sponsors
Mary Ann (coloured child) daughter of Jane & [blank] and belonging to
        Dr Geo. Moore. baptized Dec. 8th 1844 by Rev. W. M. Green.
        Billy Waddell (coloured) Sponsor
Polly Ann Jones (Adult) Wife of Dr J. B. Jones
        baptized by Rev. W. M. Green July 27th 1845: --
        Dr J. B. Jones and Mrs. Charlotte J. Green witnesses
Mary De Berniere (infant) daughter of J. B. and Polly Ann Jones
        baptized by Rev. W. M. Green July 27th 1845.
        Parents & Mrs. C. J. Green Sponsors
William Thurston (infant) son of Haynes & Mary F. Waddell
        baptized by Rev. W. M. Green July 27th 1845

_____(p. 3) _____

Baptisms (continued)

Sally Sneed – infant daughter of Rev. W^m. M. Green & Charlotte J. Green
        baptized by Bishop Ives May 24 1846.
        Parents and Mrs. Ann C. Hall Sponsors

Rebecca Garland—infant of David & Hannah Ryan
        baptized by Bishop Ives May 24th 1846.
        The Mother and Grandmother (Mrs Rebecca Lucas) Sponsors

Martha – coloured infant property of /Dr/ George Moore – daughter of Jane.
        Billy Waddell (coloured) Sponsor –
        baptized May 24th 1846 by Bishop Ives.

John Creel (adult) baptized March [blank] 1847 by W. M. Green

Edward DeBerniere – infant son of J. DeB. & Mary Hooper—
        baptized by Rev. W. M. Green April 25th 1847

Elizabeth Watters
 – infant daughter of Rev. W. M. & Charlotte J. Green
        baptized by Rev. W. M. G. April 25th 1847

Frederic
William Muhlenburg   }   sons of Manuel & Sarah Fetter – baptized April 25 1847
Henry   by Rev. Wm. M. Green –The Father Sponsor
Edward

Mrs. Caudle (adult)   baptized   [blank]   1848, by
                    Rev. A. O. Olmsted

Herbert (infant son) of Rev. W. M. Green
                    Charlotte J. Green } baptized in extremis June 30th 1848
by Rev. W. M. Green
Joel Dorsey Battle (Adult) /in sick room/ – July 16th, 1848   by Rev. W. M Green, Parents
Sponsors
Sally Cheek (adult) about Sept. 28 1848 (in extremis) by Rev. W. M. Green
Elizabeth Farrar (adult) Wife of Jefferson Farrar) private Jan. 22nd 1849
William Lucas (adult) (in extremis) Jan. 3[d] 1849 by Rev. John J. Roberts

_____(p. 4) _____

Baptisms (continued)

1849

Malvina Ferrell
Leonas Ferrell   }
Romelia Ferrell   children of Anderson & Mary Ann F.
Thomas Marion Ferrell
        baptized by Rev. W. M. Green April 20th 1849
Their mother, Mrs Hannah Ryan and Rev. T. F. Davis Sponsors
Martha Snipes, (adult, widow) by Rev. W. M. Green May 16th 1849, Rev. T. F. Davis
Sponsor

Susan ~~Caroline~~ Catharine Battle, (adult, daughter of Wm. H. & Lucy Battle)
        by Rev. W. M. Green May 16th 1849,
        her Mother + Mrs. C. J. Green, Sponsors

John Devereaux
Wesley Harvey   }
Keziah Miranda   Caudle, children of William & Sally C.
Susannah Wesley
        baptized by Rev. T. F. Davis Aug. 10th 1849
Mrs. H. Ryan + Miss S. C. Battle sponsors

Robina Norwood Mickle, bapt. by Rev. W. M. Green D.D.
        Nov. 15th (Thanksgiving Day) 1849: parents sponsors

Edward Stewart ⎤   children of Dr. J. B. & Mrs. P. A. Jones:
Symmons Baker ⎦
        by Rev. W. M. Green D. D. Nov. 16th 1849;
        parents, Miss S. Mallett & Rev. T. F. Davis Sponsors.

_____(p. 5)_____

Edith Jane (col'd) baptized in private (because of great haste to start on a long journey to the South- West) by Rev. T. F. Davis Nov 27th 1849. Child of Ellen & Andrew

Stephen, infant son of Rev. W.M. and C. J. Green,
        bapt. by Rev. T. F. Davis Dec. 17th 1849,
        parents & Mr. And. Mickle & Miss M. W. Green being Sponsors

Elizabeth Rebecca, born Jun. 30th 1845 ⎤
William Henry,   "   Jan. 29th 1847,   ⎬   of William & Sally Caudle
Peri Melissa,   "   Aug. 18th 1848 ⎦
                        bapt. July 31st 1850 by Rev. D[r] Wheat
        Sponsor Rev. T. F. Davis

Johnston Blakely, born Aug. 8th 1850   of Dr. J. B & Mrs. P. A. Jones
        bapt. Nov. 27th 1850, by Rev. T. F. Davis;
        Sponsors, parents & Rev. F. M. Hubbard & Mrs Laura Saunders

Samuel, born Sept. 29th 1850   of John & Selina Seay
        bapt. 4th Sund. after Epiph. 1851, by Rev. Dr. Wheat: Sponsors, parents & Mrs Selina Wheat

Easter Sunday ⎫ Simmons Baker—born January 27th 1851—son of Edward ⎤
April 20th   ⎬   +   ⎬ Mallett
1851.   ⎭   Mary S. ⎦
        Sponsors, with the parents, Miss Sally S. Mallett and Mr. Andrew Mickle

F.M.H.

reported to Conv. 1851

_____(p. 6)_____

Baptisms – continued

1851

July 14th   Mary Ann Brockwill – aged 12 years – in extremis – by Rev. Dr Wheat

April 3^d   Ellen Jane – daughter of J. B. Burnett – private

May 1st   Susan Rebecca daughter of Thos. W. & Mrs. Jeffries born [blank]
                 Sponsors   the mother and Mrs. Jn. H. Hubbard
                 reported to Convention of 1852

November 17   Elizabeth Nunn (Adult) By Rev. J. T. Wheat D. D.
                      <u>aged near 100 years</u>

1852

July 25th (St James')   Jane Tillinghast, born April 4th 1852, daughter of

    Mr Andrew and Mrs. Helen Mickle – The Parents– Sponsors

1853   (Since Convention)

17 July   Sally Smith (born 8th Sept. 1852) daughter
                    of Edward & Mary S. Mallett
                    Miss Sally Mallett and the parents, Sponsors

1 Dec^r   Miss Mary Amanda McDade (Adult)
                    Witnesses Mr. Mickle, Mrs. Wheat and Mrs. Battle

10 Dec^r   Henry Marsden Waddell (Adult)
                    Alfred Moore Waddell   (")
                        Witnesses: Mr. Hugh Waddell
                              Mrs. "   "
                              Mrs. Henry "
                              Miss Moore
                    Mrs. Sarah Fetter (Adult)
                    Susan Wright Fetter born August 12th 1847
                    Anna Catharine Fetter Born Nov 20th 1849
                    Martha Leggett Fetter Born Jany 30th 1853.
                        Sponsors: The Parents & Judge Battle & Mrs Battle—
                        who were also Witnesses for Mrs. F[etter]

_____(p. 7) _____

Baptisms – Continued

1854 Feb. 7   Elizabeth (coloured) daughter of Prof. Fetter's "Disey"

1854 July 9th   Simmons Baker (Born 1 April 1853) Infant
son of Dr Johnston Blakely <u>Jones</u> & his Wife
Polly Ann. Sponsors, The Parents. By J. T. W.

August 13th   Joseph Hunter (Born 28 May 1854)
Infant son of Edward and Mary Smith
<u>Mallett</u>. Sponsors, The Parents. By J. T. W.

(Omitted)

June 3rd.   Anna May (Born 7 April 1854
Infant daughter of Francis E & May
<u>Shober</u>. Sponsors The Parents & Miss
Louisa Shober.—By J. T. W

October 1st.   John Beasley (Born [blank])
Infant Son of David & Hannah <u>Ryan</u>.
Sponsors The Mother and Grand mother
Lucas.   By J. T. W.

October 21   Henry Marsden (Born 20 Sept. 1854)
Infant Son of H. M. & Elizabeth Brownrig
<u>Waddell</u>. Sponsors: Mrs. H. Waddell, Mrs.
Brownrig & Miss Sally Moore. By J. T. W.

         also

Katy, Harriet, Mary Ann, John & Egbert. Servants of Mr. Hugh Waddell.

_____(p. 8) _____

Baptisms Continued

1854

October 29   Andrew (born 28th August 1854)
              Infant Son of Andrew & Helen M. <u>Mickle</u>.
              The Parents, Sponsors

                    also

              Amy (about three years old)
              servant of Mr. Mickle.

December 20   Five Servant Children belonging
              to Miss Mary Ruffin Smith
viz.

Julius Casar aged		12
Cornelia	"	10
Emma	"	8
Annette	"	6
Laura	"	2

(The Mother's name is Harriet.)

1855

January 14.   Charles Washington (born 28 Sept. 1854)
              Infant Son of Essly & Louisa <u>Hunt</u>.
              The parents, Sponsors.

May 6.   Kemp Plummer Battle (Adult)
              His Father & Mother, <u>Witnesses</u>.

_____ **(p. 9)** _____

Baptisms Continued. by Rev. H. T. Lee

1856

Mar. 23ʳᵈ (Easter-Day.)   15 Colored Children, to Wit:
    William (belonging to Mʳ Waddell) Uncle Billy, /Sponsors/
    George (son of Jane Chavers)   mother   "
    John (belonging to Mr. Walt. Thompson) Mrs. Wheat,   "

    Horace ⎤
    Sylla   ⎬   children of Chancy /*Battle*
    Isabella ⎦   Mrs. Battle & Miss Sue Battle,   "

    Henry ⎤
    Rufus   ⎟ children of Lissy & Sam /*Morphis*/
    Sarah   ⎬   same   "
    Patsy Alice ⎟
    Ann Elisa ⎦

    Margaret ⎤
    Fanny Green ⎬ children of Jane /*Battle*/
    Annie Swain ⎦   same   "

    Edward Plummer, son of Judy /& *Tom Kirby*/
                Same   "
June 8 (3ᵈ S. aft. Trinity
            1 Adult. to wit: Jane, servant of Mrs. Shober. Witnesses Mrs. Shober & Mrs
Wheat
                (by Rev. J. T. Wheat D. D.)

August 10 (12 Sun. aft. Trinity)
    Johnston Jones: infant son of Edward & Mary S. Mallett   by H. T. L.
            Sponsors: Parents, and Dr. J. B. Jones

_____ (p. 10) _____

1856   Baptisms Continued

August 11 (Monday Evening) Privately.

> Edward Lazarus: aged 4 years /(sick)/: + Florence Nightengale: aged 1 year;
> infant Children of [blank] Mrs Martha Perkins
> > Sponsors: The Mother: + Mrs. Selina Wheat

1857: Feb. 8. Sept^a Sunday.

> > Helen Mary infant daughter of Andrew & Helen Mickle
> Aged 2 Months.   Sponsors: The Parents

April 10. Good Friday. Mrs Martha Perkins
> > > Witnesses: Mr Andrew Mickle & W. A. Thompson
"   "   3 Children of Mrs. Perkins
> > > Andrew Jackson: aged 11 years
> > > David Washington: "   7   "
> > > Lucretia Emmaline: "   5   "
> > > > Sponsor: The Mother

July 19. Col^d infant Emily: belonging to Rector, aged 8 mo.
> > Sponsor: Mrs Lee

" " Col^d girl Maria: daughter of Milly; belonging to Mr. E. Mallett; aged 5 years
> > Sponsor: The Grandmother Hannah.

Oct. 4. 17th Sund. aft. Trin.

> > Annie Stewart: infant daughter
> of Dr. Johnston Blakeley, & Polly Ann Jones.
> > Sponsors: The Parents, & Miss Maria Spear

_____ **(p. 11)** _____

1857   Baptisms Continued

Nov. 29. Advent Sunday   Frederick Stanton: infant son of Richard & Mary Saunders
                              Sponsors: Parents, & Wm L. Saunders.

1858

Easter Day. Apr. 4.
        Thomas Nash Cameron   infant son of
        Dr. William Peter & Caroline De Ber. Mallett
                              Sponsors: Parents

12 September 1858: Infant daughter of Ed. & Mary Mallett
        Martha Green, born 22 June 1858
        (Parents, Sponsors)   By J. T. Wheat

        Adult: 17 October 1858.
                Edward Hugh Davis of Elizabeth City
                        Messrs. Walker Anderson
                                Geo Johnston   Witnesses
        By J. T. Wheat

        Adult: 23 October 1858
                Augustus Moore Flythe of Northampton Co.
                        Messrs. Geo. Martin
                        F. A. Fetter,   Witnesses
        By J. T. Wheat

_____(p. 12) _____

Baptisms by Rev E M Forbes 1859

July 17th John /(born April 15 1859)/ Parents and Sponsors Andrew & Helen Mickle

Sep 5th Sylvia (colored) servant to Mr & Mrs Mickle who were sponsors

Sep   Parthenia ⎤
"   Maria Spear ⎦ servants of Miss Mary Smith

Nov. 9th Lissie (Infant) /born Oct. 1859/ Parents & Sponsors H. & M B Smith with Mrs. Hoke

1860

April 5 William Laurence (Infant) Parents + Sponsors Mr. & Mrs Richard Saunders /with Mrs. Jos. Saunders/

October 7th William Murdoch (Infant) Parents & Sponsors Dr Wm & Mrs DB Mallett

March 28 1863- By Bp. Atkinson – Ellen daughter of S. J. and Ellen Person- born 17th Feb 1863

June 26 1861 - By Rev F. W. Hilliard – Laura Baker, infant child of R. B. /& Mary/ Saunders –

June 26 1861 – Charles Earl, Infant Child of Geo. B. & Nannie T. Johnston, by the same

4th Aug 1861 – By Rev. F. W. Hilliard – Lewis, Sam, Jesse, Margaret – col[d] children, belonging to D[r] W[m] P. Mallett.

Sept 1st 1861 – By Rev. F W. Hilliard, Junius, Col[d] Infant, belonging to H. H. Smith

March 17th 1862 – By Rev. F. W. Hilliard – William Hight, infant son of E. H & Julia B. Davis –

April 13th 1862 – James Washington Reed – infant by Rev. F. W. H.

April 20th 1862 – Thomas Manney – infant son of John Kimberly & Bettie, his wife. By Rev. F. W. Hilliard –

May 11th 1862.   By Rev F. W. Hilliard - Nancy Perkins, white adult.

_____(p. 13) _____

Baptisms

May 14th 1862 – By Rev. F. W. Hilliard –William Lowndes Quarles – White adult–
Witness M. M. Marshall.

June 15th 1862 By Rev. F. W. Hilliard – Jim – Colored Child, belonging to R. B. Saunders-

July 17th 1862 - By Rev. S. J. Johnston D. D. Samuel Iredell Johnston, son of Rev. F. W. &
Maria N. Hilliard, aged 2 m[os] and 6 days – Sponsors – D[r] Johnston – George and Nannie
Johnston –

Aug. 10th 1862 - By Rev. F. W. Hilliard – David Blount – col[d] child, belonging to F. W.
Hilliard –

Aug. 17th 1862 - By Rev. F. W. Hilliard – Susan, colored infant, belonging to A. Mickle.

Oct. 6th 1862 - By Rev. F. W. Hilliard – Jennie Woodhouse, infant daughter of Dr. W. P. &
/Mrs./ De Berniere Mallet –

June 2nd 1863 – Edward Hugh, Infant Son of E. H. & Julia B. Davis -
by Rev. F. W. Hilliard –

July 19th 1863. John – Son of John & Bettie Kimberly by Rev. F. W. Hilliard –

Aug. 9th 1863 - By Rev. F. W. Hilliard Esther Cotton, col[d] child belonging to F. W. Hilliard,
and Albert Sidney, col[d] child, belonging to S. I. Johnston.

_____(p. 14) _____

Baptisms

Aug. 23rd 1863 – By Rev. F. W. Hilliard – Caroline Daley – daughter of D[r] J. B. and Polly
Ann Jones – aged 18 mo's

Oct 11th 1863 - Elizabeth Brandon, daughter of R. B. & Mary Saunders – aged 6 mo's –
Sponsors – the parents and Mrs. Laura Saunders – by Rev. F. W. Hilliard

Nov. 22nd 1863. Lucy Battle col[d] child belonging to Miss Mary Smith. Sponsor, Miss Mary
Smith. – By Rev. F. W. Hilliard –

April 3rd 1864 – Annie, cold infant, belonging to A. R. Elliott – By Rev. F. W. Hilliard -

April 13th 1864 – By Rev. F. W. Hilliard – David Moore, free colored adult- Witness John, Servt of A. J. De Rosset –

April 24th 1864 – By Rev. F. W. Hilliard – Cornelius Burnet, free cold adult- Witness, Andrew Mickle

May 29th 1864 – By Rev. F. W. Hilliard – George Johnston, infant son of Rev F. W. & Maria N. Hilliard aged 1 mo. & 26 days. Sponsors – the Father, John Johnston and Nannie T. Johnston -

Sept. 11th 1864 – By Rev. F. W. Hilliard. Catharine Davis, daughter of Dr. M. J. and Ada De Rosset, aged 1 mo. & 16 days – Sponsors- Thos. Mears – Mrs. Catharine Mears (the elder) and Mrs. Gaston H. Mears.

_____(p. 15) _____

Baptisms

Sept. 27th 1864 – By Rev. F. W. Hilliard – Bailey Shelby – infant son of E. H. and Julia B. Davis

Oct. 9th 1864 – By Rev. F. W. Hilliard – Amy – colored infant, belonging to Jos. H. Pool

Oct. 6th 1864 – By Rev. F. W. Hilliard – Robert Burton, aged 3 weeks, son of H. H. & Mary B. Smith

Oct. 16th 1864 – By Rev. F. W. Hilliard – Mary – aged 4 mo's, daughter of John and Bettie Kimberly –

Oct. 23rd 1864 – By Rev. F. W. Hilliard – George – belonging to Wm A. Wright, Mary, George, Ida, belonging to C. P. Mallett, col'd infants –

Oct. 30th 1864 – Cora, Washington, & Robert Lewis, col'd children, belonging to W. H. Battle, by Rev. F. W. Hilliard –

Nov. 6th 1864 – By Rev. F. W. Hilliard – Mary Banister, daughter of Dr. Wm H. & Fannie Morrow, aged 4 Mo's – Sponsors- Dr J. B. Jones, Mrs. De B. Mallett – and Madame Gouze

_____(p. 16) _____

Baptisms

Dec. 3rd 1864 - By Rev. F. W. Hilliard—Edward aged 6 weeks, son of Dr Edward & Elizabeth Cotton Warren—Sponsors: Gabriel Johnston, Mrs. Eliza N. Thompson & Mrs. Nannie T. Johnston –

May 22nd 1865 – By Rev. F. W. Hilliard—Mary /(Varina)*/ infant daughter of R.B. Saunders and Mary, his wife. Sponsors—W. L. Saunders Mrs. Laura Saunders, & Miss Ann Saunders–

/* added by me Jos. Blount Cheshire Jr. Apl. 21/ 79/

1867

July 14th Florida Cotton and Joseph Hubbard, twin children of Richard B. and Mary Saunders—born [blank]

Sponsors: Col. Wm L and Miss Anne Saunders

Sept. 29th Samuel infant child (coloured) of Henry and Emma Morfis

The Mother & [blank] Sponsors

_____(p. 17) _____

May 19th 1878

1878

By Jos. Blount Cheshire Jr. Deacon. Richard Henry, infant son of Dr. Richard H. Lewis, and Cornelia Viola, his wife, the sponsors being the parents, the grand-parents (Mr. and Mrs. Kemp P. Battle), and the great-grand father Hon. Wm H. Battle. The child was born Feb. 18th 1878.

May 27th. At the house of Mr. Wm L. Wall in Durham /by the same/. William Lewis, infant son of Wm L. Wall and Catharine S. his wife in presence of a congregation there assembled.

The Sponsors were the parents, Mrs. Mercer, the grandmother, and Col. Robert F. Webb. The child was born Apl. 8th 1878.

1879

April 13th Easter day—Chapel of the Cross

Walter Everett Phillips, student in the University of N. C. from Edgecombe County, son of late Dr. J. J. Phillips; nat. July 17 1800

Henry Laurence Battle. Student in University from Edgecombe County, son of J. J. Battle; natus Dec. 14th 1862.

The Witnesses being Hon. Kemp. P. Battle and Frank B. Davey. By Jos. Blunt Cheshire Jr. Deacon ministering in this parish.

May 28th. Chapel of the Cross by Jos. Blount Cheshire Jr. Deacon
Ellen Hale, born Apl. 4th 1877
William Laurence born Nov. 25th 1874
Infant daughter and Son of Richard B. Saunders and Mary his wife: Sponsors, the Parents and Miss Anne Saunders

_____(p. 18) _____

1879

Aug. 24th 11th Sunday after Trinity. Chapel of the Cross

Martha Battle, born Mch. 22d 1879 infant daughter
of Dr. Rich. H. Lewis and Cornelia Viola his wife of Raleigh. Sponsors the parents, the grandmothers (Mrs. Martha E. Lewis & Mrs. Kemp P. Battle) and Kemp P. Battle Jr.

By Jos. Blount Cheshire D.D.

Elizabeth Toole, born July 2d 1879. infant daughter of Jos. Blount Cheshire Jr. and Annie Huske his wife. Sponsors the parents, and maternal /(?)/ grandmother (Mrs. J. B. Cheshire Sr.) and Mrs. Rich. H. Lewis.

By Jos. Blount Cheshire D.D.

Oct. 5th Seventeenth Sunday after Trinity

At the residence of Claudius A. W. Barham, Durham N.C.,
<u>Jethro Ballard</u>, infant son of Claudius A. W. Barham and Alexina G. his wife.
Born Nov. 30th 1878. Sponsors, the mother, grand-mother, Mrs. Raiford, and
Jos. Blount Cheshire Jr.

> By Jos. Blount Cheshire Jr.
> Deacon

1880

Feb. 1st Sexagesima Sunday. At the residence of James N. Gammon in the Town of
Durham, in presence   of a congregation of /Christian people/

> 1. <u>James Norfleet</u> Gammon. Adult son of Wiley Gammon and Emily his wife late of
> Halifax County, N.C. born May 31st 1850. Witnesses, William L. Wall, and Col.
> Rob't F. Webb.

> Also at same time and place

> 2. <u>Mary Norfleet</u>, infant daughter of /sd/ James N Gam-

_____(p. 19) _____

1880

> -mon and Josephine S. his wife, born Feb. 19th 1879. Sponsors. Col. Rob't F.
> Webb, Mrs. R. F. Webb & Mrs. Claude B. Hooker.

By Jos. Blount Cheshire Jr. Deacon.

March 7th Fourth Sunday in Lent. At the residence of
Mr. Henry M. Rosemond in presence of a congregation of Christian people.
Robert Thomas, infant son of Henry M. and Dora Palmer Rosemond, born June 23^d 1879.
Sponsors Col. Robert F. Webb, Spencer W. Chamberlain and Mrs. Spencer W. Chamberlain.

> By Jos. Blount Cheshire Jr. Deacon

Sept. 26th. Eighteenth Sunday after Trinity. At the residence of Mr. DeWitt C. Mangum in
presence of a congregation of Christian people there assembled

> DeWitt Clifton, born Jany. 25th 1878

Olga Paola, born Dec. 25th 1879

Infant Son and daughter of DeWitt C. and Matilda M. Mangum: The Parents being the only Sponsors.

By Jos. Blount Cheshire Jr. Priest in charge of Miss. Station.

1881 Feb. 27th. Quinquagesima. At the residence of Col. Robert F. Webb, in the town of Durham, in the presence of a congregation of Christian people, there assembled,

Mary Amanda, born Feb. 11th 1880.

infant daughter of Charles E. Crabtree and Virginia A. his wife, the parents and Col. Rob't F. Webb and Mrs. Henrietta J. Webb, being S[p]onsors.

by Jos. Blount Cheshire Jr.
Priest in charge of Mission

_____ (pp. 20-27 blank) _____

Confirmations

1858

24 October. Twenty First Sunday after Trinity
By Rt. Revd Bp. Atkinson, Diocesan.
Presented by J. T. Wheat (Officiating Pro. tem.)

Hildreth Smith	Leonidas Polk Wheat
Richard Saunders	Augustus Moore Flythe
Frederick Augustus Fetter	John Routh Bowie
Hugh Hazzart Bein	Isaac Augustus Jarratt
Lawrence Mel Anderson	Arthur Nelson McKimmon
Thomas Capehart	George Saunders Martin
Richard Cogdell Badger	George Pettigrew Bryan
Thomas S Armistead	

and

Susan Holden; a free, coloured woman.

April 25th 1864 —
Bishop Thos. Atkinson D.D. L.L.D. Rector F. W. Hilliard

S. Garland Ryan	Lydia Van Wyck
John S. Henderson	Kate Fetter
Herbert Mallett	Florence Wright
Wm. A. Wright Jr.	Robena Mickle
Henry A. London Jr.	
Iredell Johnston	

_____(p. 28) _____

Confirmations — Continued [from text on p. 83]

Jos. Blount Cheshire Jr.
Deacon Ministering in this parish

Jos. Augustus Williams, of Chatham	County	
Jos. ~~Summer~~omerville Cunningham, of Person	do.	
Walter Everett Phi/l/lips, of Edgecombe	do.	
Henry Laurence Battle of do.	do,	
Jos. Carey Dowd " do.	do.	Students in University
Frank Battle Dancey " do.	do.	
Francis Gordon Hines " Chowan	do.	
Alfred Abraham Kent " Caldwell	do.	
Herbert Bemerton Battle, of Chapel Hill		

Elizabeth Brandon Saunders
Mary Varina Saunders

By Rt. Rev. Theo. B. Lyman, D. D.
May 8th 1879

Zeno Brown of Pitt County
Herbert Ward Pender, of Edgecombe do.
Students in Un. by the Rt. Rev.
Thos. Atkinson, D.D., L.L.D. (Cantab.)
Nov. 9th (22^d Sunday after Trinity) 1879

In a public hall at Durham
James Norfleet Gammon
Josephine Samuella Gammon
Claude Virginia Claypoole Barham   Feb. 1st 1880
Dora Palmer Rosemond   Sexagesima Sunday
          by Theodore B. Lyman, D.D.
(one page <u>back</u>)   Apt. Bishop of Diocese

_____(p. 29) _____

Confirmations

Archibald [McLean crossed out] *Maclaine* Hooper ⎱
Mary Hooper ⎰ Sept. 27th, 1843
Edward Hubbel Hicks

Catharine Waddell ⎱
Elizabeth Waddell
Rosa /Troy/ Hall ⎰ May 24th 1846
James S. Green
James F. Waddell

Joel D. Battle ⎱
Susan C. Battle
Francenious Ferrell
James M. Johnson ⎰ May 19th 1849
Polly Ann Jones
Joseph A. Manning
Martha Snipes
Mary Ann Ferrell (being sick) privately,
   May 19th 1849

Richard Hines (of Raleigh) ⎱ Jan. 28th 1850
Lawrence Smith (of parish of /Trinity Church Scotl. Neck/) ⎰

_____(p. 30) _____

Confirmations

1854

19 February – Sexagesima Sunday

       By Rt. Rev. Thomas Atkinson D.D.
                              Diocesan
Presented by J. T. Wheat   R[ecto]r of the parish

Alfred Moore Waddell
Henry Marsden Waddell
William Harding Moore
Joseph Bibb Lucas
John Hines
Jno. Husk Tillinghast
Mrs. Sarah Fetter
" Rosanna Jeffries
Miss /Mary/ Amanda McDade
" Anne Saunders
Mrs. Mary Paxton   (11.)

1854

Nov[r] 10   Thomas /S./ Hill, a student from Wilmington

Presented by Rev. H. T. Lee

1856. July 27

D[r] Johnston Blakely Jones
Richardson Mallett

1857. May 8   By the Same:

Mrs. Martha Perkins

1858. Mar. 21   By the Same:

Jas. M. Henderson & wife
Mary De Berniere Jones

_____(p. 31) _____

Confirmations.

1858

24 October. Twenty First Sunday after Trinity

By Rt. Rev[d] Bp. Atkinson, Dioscesan

Presented by J. T. Wheat (Officiating Pro. Tem.)

Hildreth Smith
Richard Saunders
Frederick Augustus Fetter
Hugh Hagart Bein
Lawrence Mel Anderson
Thomas Capehart
Richard Cogdell Badger
Thomas S   Armistead

Leonidas Polk Wheat
Augustus Moore Flythe
John Routh Bowie
Isaac Augustus Jarratt
Arthur Nelson McKimmon
George Saunders Martin
George Pettigrew Bryan

and

Susan Holden; a free, coloured woman.

1859

Nov.

Junius Battle
Joseph Saunders
Woodson L Garrett
Rebekah Bryan
Margaret Mallett.

1865, August 31st   Virginius St. Clair McNider

_____(p. 32) _____

Confirmations

May 15th 1862.

Bishop - Thomas Atkinson D.D. -- Rector. Francis W. Hilliard

William N. Mickle
Joseph Mickle
Wm L. Quarles

Mrs. Mary J. Van Wyck
Annie Mickle
Sophy Mallett

June 5th 1862

Bishop. Thos. Atkinson D.D. L.L.D.   Rector F. W. Hilliard

Wm W. Jones   Nancy Perkins
Albert M. Boozer

March 28th 1863

Bishop. Thos. Atkinson D.D. L.L.D.   Rector. F. W. Hilliard

Thos. M. Argo   Lucy Whitaker
Aug. Van Wyck

                Albina Mears ⎤
                Margaret Smith ⎦ colored

_____(p. 33) _____

Confirmations

April 25th 1864

Bishop Thos. Atkinson D.D. L.L.D.   Rector F. W. Hilliard

S. Garland Ryan   Lydia Van Wyck
John S. Henderson   Kate Fetter
Herbert Mallett   Florence Wright
Wm. A Wright Jr.   Robina Mickle
Henry A. London Jr.
Iredell Johnston
Andrew Perkins

           David Moore   ⎤
           Cornelius Burnet
           Laura Smith   ⎬ Colored
           Emma Smith
           Eliza Mallett ⎦

July 21ˢᵗ 1868,   by Rt. Rev. Thomas Atkinson

Miss Susan Davis

F. M. Hubbard, minister in charge

1877

Nov. 20   by Rt. Rev. Thos. Atkinson – Robert B. Sutton in charge

John M. Manning of Pittsborough
James S. Manning   "
Robᵗ Strange of Wilmington   Students in the
Ernest Haywood of Raleigh   University of N. C.
James /H./ Ruffin of Hillsborough

(Record of Confirmations continues from this date five pages back
                              J. B. C., Jr.).

Marriages

Marriages: by Rev. H. T. Lee.

On the evening of the 10th June. 1856. Thos. K. Emory of New bern, & Julia Rebecca, daughter of Dr. Geo. J. Moore of Chapel Hill.

16 September 1858: by J. T. Wheat, John R. Clements and Nancy E. Hester of Orange County.

Dec 28 1859 Major Carr (colored) to Margaret Smith (colored)

August 23, 1865.   Brig. Gen. Smith D. Atkins, of Freeport, Illinois, to Miss Eleanor H. Swain, daughter of Gov. D. L. Swain.
F. M. Hubbard

1866
Sept. 27th Wilson Caldwell to Susan Kirby. (both colored)
F. M. H.

_____(p. 34) _____

Marriages

Lucian Holmes
Mary S. /Shaw/ Mitchell`   *2nd or 3rd Nov 1847 by W M Green*

Charles Phillips
Laura /C./ Battle   ~~*7th or*~~ *8th Dec 1847 by W M Green*

Samuel F. Phillips
Frances Lucas   Dec. 4th 1849, by Rev. W. M. Green D. D.
(the lady being of our congregation)

Henry Marsden Waddell
Elizabeth [blank] Brownrig   By J. T. W. [on 24 Sept. 1853—from marriage certificate]

_____(p. 35) _____

Marriages

Sam (Morfis)
Lizzy (Battle)   *coloured*

Henry (Weaver)
Celia (Green)   *coloured*   *July 19th 1845*

Washington (Snipes)
Jane (Battle)   *coloured*   *June 12 1847*

Andrew (Moore[?])
Ellen (Green)   *col^d*   *Jan 1848   by Rev. W M Green*

Tom (Small)

            col^d   *Sept   1848   by W M Green*

Margaret (Lucas)

Tom (Kirby)

                            Oct 5th 1848   by W. M. Green

Judy (Battle)

William

   &   Jones, (coloured,) Dec. 27th 1849, by Rev. T. F. Davis: both

Henrietta   of them being unbaptized

Lawrence (belonging to Ed. Mallett)   8 Sept.

   &   1855

Annie (belonging to Hugh Waddell)

                       By <u>J. T. W.</u>

_____(p. 36)_____

Marriages: by Rev. H. T. Lee

On the evening of the 10th June. 1856 Thos. R. Emery of New Bern, & Julia Rebecca, daughter of Dr Geo. J. Moore of Chapel Hill.

16 September 1858: by J. T. Wheat, John R. Clements and Nancy E. Hester. of Orange County

Dec. 28 1859 Major Carr (colored) to Margaret Smith (colored)

<u>August 23^d, 1865.</u> Brig. Gen. Smith D. Atkins, of Freeport, Illinois,
                 to Miss Eleanor H. Swain, daughter of Gov. D. L. Swain.
                      F. M. Hubbard

Sept. 27th /1866/   Wilson Caldwell to Susan Kirby (both coloured)
                      F. M. H.

_____(p. 37) _____

Marriages

July 24th 1861 – By Rev. F. W. Hilliard – William
   Van Wyck & Mary J. Battle

   1863 – By Rev. J. H. Wingfield. – S. Edward
   Hines & Louisa Pool

May 25th 1864. By Rev. F. W. Hilliard – Thomas
   M. Argo & Martha H. Hubbard

June 2nd 1864. By Rev. F. W. Hilliard – John
   Buxton Williams & Carrie V. Peters

Dec. 22nd 1864 – Henry Servant of W. H. Battle &
   Emma " " Mary Smith –
   By — Rev. F. W. Hilliard

June 21st 1877. Prof. Ralph /*Henry*/ Graves to Julia C. Hooper both of
   Chapel Hill. – at the residence of Prof. J. DeB. Hooper –
   By Robt B. Sutton in charge –

Nov. 13th 1878. Oliver M. Royster of Hickory son of the late Marcus
   D. Royster of Granville County to Martha G. Mallett of
   this place, daughter of the late Col. Ed. Mallett at the
   Chapel of the Cross by Jos. Blount Cheshire Jr. Deacon ministering in this church.

Sept. 7th 1880 Charles Beatty of Va. to Kate R. Wampler
   also of Va. in the Methodist Church. in Durham
   by Jos. Blount Cheshire Jr. Minister in Charge
   of St. Philip's Mission Station, Durham

_____(pp. 38-41, [41a-b], 42 blank) _____

_____(p. 43 tipped in, typewritten) _____

The Vestry of the Chapel of the Cross, Chapel Hill, on the resignation of the Rector of the Parish, Rev. Dr. Homer Worthington Starr, place on record their deep sense of the value of his services to the Parish. He has been punctual to all duties, an able and instructive preacher, prompt and effectual in attention to the sick and the afflicted. He has been careful in keeping his congregation well informed as to their duties in regard to Missions, organized and instructed Bible classes, and enlarged our Sunday school; has given careful instruction to Confirmation Classes, worked with the St. Andr[ews] Brotherhood and the Young Men's Christian Association, in truth was singularly active in endeavors to arouse interest in the work of the Church. His efforts to interest and influence our students in the direction of sound morals and love of Christ have been constant and untiring.

It was by the energetic stimulus of Dr. Starr that a beautiful and commodious Parish House has been added to our Church Building, and a handsome and convenient /Rectory/ erected. He crowned his labors by the successful inauguration of a vested choir, adding much to the devotional spirit and beauty of the music.

For the intelligence, the energy, the perseverance, the kindliness, and devotion Dr. Starr has shown while our Rector, the Vestry feel deeply grateful and spread this record on the minutes of the Parish, and send a copy thereof to him, with our earnest wish for his future happiness and success in his new duties.

K. P. Battle
Chas. H. Healy   Committee
G. Kenneth G. Henry
April 13ᵗʰ 1916   J. S. Holmes

_____(p. 44-45 blank) _____

Funerals

1861
Oct – 13 – Sarah, servant of John Walker
Oct. 27 – Dena, daughter of Dr. W. P. and Dr. B. Mallett

1863 –
March 14th Bob, servt. of H. H. Smith –
March 31st Margaret, servt. of H. H. Smith –
Aug – 6th Nellie, infant daughter of S. J. & Ellen Person
Aug 29th Lieut. Richardson Mallett –
Sept 3rd Thomas Haney of Pasquotank Co. N. C.
Sept 8th Juno, Servant of G. B. Johnston –
Sept 18th Edward Hugh, child of E. H. & J. B. Davis

1864
June 8th Edward Stuart Jones, son of Dr. J. B. & Polly Jones –
1865 –
March 25 – Lieut Col. Edward Mallett –

1865 Sept. 2, Maria – a colored girl, at Dr. DeRosett's.
   " 9th Mrs Polly Anne Jones, wife of Dr. Johnson B. Jones.
   " Dec. 6th Mrs Mary Mallett, widow of Col. Edward Mallett: in the absence
1866 of the minister ~~~~ parish the funeral service was read by Judge Battle.
April 16th

1866
May 14th Dr James William Brandon Greenhow: aged 51 years, Fleet Surgeon in
      the Navy of the Confederate States.
1867. March 3 Mrs Sarah Fetter: wife of Prof. Manuel Fetter of the University.
   "   "   29th Miss Anne C. Swain, eldest daughter of Hon. David L. Swain,
      the President of the University.   F. M. Hubbard

_____(p. 46) _____

Funerals

Tory (col'd woman, not of our congregation) by Rev. W. M. Green D.D. Nov. 4th 1849

(little col'd girl, not baptized) by Rev. W. M. Green D. D. Nov. 25th 1849

1852
Feb. 7th   Thos W. Jeffreys (funeral service by Rev. J. T. Wheat D. D,)
April 6th 7th   Mr Thomas Lloyd Moore – one of the Wardens of this parish
Nov. 9th   Hon. James S. Smith, M. D. *aged 66 years*

1853
July 16   An infant son of Burnet (colored.)

1854
Feb. 7   An infant (Elizabeth) slave of Mr. Fetter
April 21   Henry Marsden Waddell Esq. (Aged 25 years.)
Nov. 10   Mrs. Delia Smith (widow of Dr J. S. Smith)

1855
10 Oct.   William, servant of Dr Jones
               Attended by Rev. H. T. Lee

1856
Aug. 15   Edward Lazarus, infant son of Mrs. [blank] Perkins
Nov. 2   Col'd infant at Mr. Edwd Mallett's plantation
Dec. 30   Col'd girl, aged 14. named Martha, belonging to Dr Moore, from Mr. Fetter's,

1857
1st Apr.   (Rev. J. T. Wheat. D.D.) The funeral of Dr Geo. J. Moore, at Pittsboro.
14th Dec.   Col'd girl – Frances, – belonging to Govr Swain.

1858
July 20.   Funeral of Cameron, infant son of Dr W. P. Mallett,   attd by Dr. Wheat.
  " 23.   "   Mr Jos. B. Lucas, a Communicant of C. of Cross.   do. do.
Nov. 24   "   Dr Joel Battle, eldest son of Hon. Wm Battle do. do.

1859
Oct 13   [blank]

_____(p. 47) _____

Funerals.

1865   Sept. 2   Maria – a coloured girl, at Dr. De Rosset's.
        " 9th   Mrs Polly Anne Jones, wife of Dr. Johnson B. Jones
"   Dec. 6th   Mrs Mary Mallett, widow of Col. Edward Mallett: in the absence of
the Minister of the parish the funeral service was read by Judge Battle.

1866
April 16th   [blank]

1866
May 14th   Dr James William Brandon Greenhow: aged 51 years, Fleet Surgeon
                        in the Navy of the Confederate States
1867 March 3rd   Mrs Sarah Fetter: – wife of Prof. Manuel Fetter of the University
"   "   29th   Miss Anne C. Swain: — eldest daughter of Hon. David L. Swain, the
                        President of the University.   F. M. Hubbard

1861
Oct. 13 –   Sarah, Servant of John Walker
Oct. 27 –   Dena, daughter of Dr W. P. and De B. Mallett

1863
March 14th   Bob, servant of H. H. Smith
March 31st   Margaret, servant of H. H. Smith
Aug. 6th   Nellie, infant daughter of S. J. & Ellen Person
Aug. 29th   Lieut. Richardson Mallett
Sept. 3rd   Thomas Harvey of Pasquotank Co. N.C.
Sept. 8th   Juno, Servant of G. B. Johnston
Sept. 18th   Edward Hugh, child of E. H. & J. B. Davis

1864
June 8th   Edward Stuart Jones, son of Dr. J. B. & Polly Jones

1865
March 25   Lieut Col. Edward Mallett —

_____(p. 48) _____

Funerals-

July 10th 1865-   Mrs. Florida, wife of Col. W. L. Saunders

1867 April 22^d – M^{rs} [blank]
     May 12th   Anna Aske Emery, infant
     Sept. 22^d Miss Susan C. Battle, the last surviving daughter of Hon. W. H. Battle
                                               F.M.H.

1868   Jan. 5th Mrs Martha Snipes

1878   Feb. 21   Jane T. Mickle daughter of Andrew & Helen Mickle
                   in Public Cemetery from the Church. by Rob. B. Sutton in charge
       Nov. 24th Louis Phelps and Theodore Lyman (ages 5 & 3 years), infant children of
                   Col. Robert F. Webb and wife of Durham: buried in the public
                   cemetery near Durham from the residence of Col. Webb in that
                   town, Jos. Blount Cheshire Jr. Deacon

1879
 Nov. 16th   William Lewis (aged 1 yr. 7 mos. 8 days) infant son of Wm L. Wall & wife of
                 Durham in the public cemetery near Durham, from the residence of W^m L.
                 Wall in that town, by Jos. Blount Cheshire Jr. Deacon

1880
Oct. 13th   Wiley Williams Grist (aged 3 years 7 mos. 15 days) infant son of Allan Grist
                 and wife, in the public cemetery at Chapel Hill, from the residence of the
                 parents, the child having died with diphtheria. by Jos. Blount Cheshire Jr.

Oct. 31st   Miss Ann Judith Monroe, a native of the Island
                 of St. Thomas, West Indies, aged 57 years, 9 months, & 18 days.
                 Funeral Services from the Chapel of the Cross, burial in the
                 public Cemetery, by Jos. Blount Cheshire Jr.

_____(p. 49) _____

Jany 7th 1881
    Miss Maria Louisa Speer aged 76 years,
             died Jany 5th 1880 at residence of Miss Mary R. Smith.
             Orange County. Buried at the Smith Family Bury-
             ing Ground, Jones's Grove, Chatham County by
             the Rev. Edmund N. Joyner of St. Bartholomew's
             Church, Pittsboro, in the absence of the Rector of
             this Parish.

_____(pp. 50-59 blank) _____

_____(p. 60) _____

1880   Bishop's Assessment and Convention Fund

| Name | Amt. assessed | Payments 1880-1881 | | | | 1881-1882 | | | |
		July 1.	Oct. 1.	Jany. 1.	Apl. 1.	June 30.	Sept. 30	Dec. 31.	Mch. 31.
Mr. Battle	1.25	1.25	1.25	1.25	1.25				
Miss M. Smith	1.00	1.00	1.00	1.00	1.00				
Mrs. Taylor	.75	.75	.75	.75	.75				
Mr. Hooper	.75	.75	.75	75	.75				
Dr. Mallett	.50	.50	.50	.50	.50				
Mr. Mickell	.50	.50	.50	.50	.50				
Mrs. Saunders	.50	.50	.50	.50	.50				
Mrs. Cheshire	.50	.50	.50	.50	.50				
Mrs. Graves	.25	.25	.25	.25	.25				
Mrs. Barbee	.25	.25	.25	.25	.25				
xMiss Maria Speer	.25	.25	.25	dead					
Mr. Winston	.25	.25	.25	.25	.25				
	6.75	6.75	6.75	6.50	6.50				

6.75
6.50
6.50   Assesssment
26.50   for year End-
25.   ing Mch. 31 -81
1.50   balance pd.
        to Mr. Joyner
        June 24 -81

July 1 – pd. $8-   Oct. 1. pd. $6   Jany 1- pd $7.00   Mch. 26 $6.50   = returned $2.50

_____(p. 61 blank) _____

_____(p. 62) _____

Jos. Blount Cheshire Jr., Rector, in Act. with the Chapel of the Cross

Communion Alms		Dr.	Cr.
1880	June 20	$2.18	St. Martins
	July 18	3.58	Ch. Hamilton – 3.00
	Aug. 15	2.84	To Sarah Barbee
			sick and destitute 1.00
	Oct. 3ᵈ	2.72	Parish Register 8.45
	Nov. 7ᵗʰ	2.41	Printing Cards 3.50
1881	Feb. 6ᵗʰ	2.71	
	Apl. 3ᵈ	2.45	
	May 1	2.11	

_____(p. 63) _____

Contributions to extra-parochial objects

1878				
	June 2ⁿᵈ	Diocesan Missions	23.34	
	Dec. 15ᵗʰ	Domestic Missions	18.60	
	1879 Jany. 26ᵗʰ	Foreign Missions	18.75	
	Feb. 16ᵗʰ	Diocesan Missions, Bps' visitation	14.00	
	May 8ᵗʰ	Diocesan Missions, Bps' visitation	11.00	85.69
1879				
	June 29ᵗʰ	Regular Quarterly Con. to Diocesan Missions	10.00	
	Sept. 28ᵗʰ	do. do. do. do.	15.03	
	Nov. 9ᵗʰ	Bp's Visitation do. do.	11.44	
	" 27ᵗʰ	Thanks-giving Day		
		for Oxford Orphan Asylum	15.00	
	Dec. 21ˢᵗ	Domestic Missions, Advent offering	18.25	
1880	Jany. 18ᵗʰ	Epiphany Offering for Foreign Missions	18.81	88.53
	March 28ᵗʰ	Easter Day. Quarterly offering for		
		Diocesan Missions	20.00	108.53
	June 27ᵗʰ	5ᵗʰ Sunday after Trinity. Quarterly offering		
		for Diocesan Missions 1ˢᵗ quarter	22.26	

	Sept. 5th	15 S. after Trinity 2nd Quarterly Offering for Diocesan Missions	19.00
	Nov. 25th	Thanksgiving Day. Offering for the Oxford Orphan Asylum	9.00
	Dec. 5th	2nd Sunday in Advent. 3rd quarterly offering Dioc. Miss.	11.00
1881	Mch. 6th	1st Sunday in Lent 4th do. do. do.	15.51
	May 11th	2 quarters' Missionary subscription this day remitted to Dr. A. T. Twyng Treas. Domestic C...	43.00

_____ (pp. 64-83) _____

[Modern index of names; not transcribed here]

Communicants

Communicants
of
the Church in the Parish
of the
Chapel of the Cross
at the Diocesan Convention of 1848-9.

Rev. W. M. Green:	Removed to Miss. Dec. 1849.
Mrs. C. I. Green:	Removed to Miss. Dec. 1849.
Miss M. W. Green:	Removed to Miss. Dec. 1849
Rev. F. M. Hubbard:	Removed. 1852
Mrs. Martha H. Hubbard:	
Judge W. H. Battle:	
Mrs. Lucy Battle:	
Mrs. Laura Phillips:	Decided to Presbyterians Sept. -49
Mrs. Rebecca Lucas:	
Mrs. Hannah Ryan:	
Miss Sally S. Mallett:	
Mr. John M. Craig:	
Mrs. Elizabeth Craig:	
Miss Matilda Williams:	
Mr. A. M. Hooper:	Removed July -49.
Mrs. C. Hooper:	Removed July 1849.
Mr. Lloyd Moore:	died April 6th 1852
Mr. T. D. Haigh (student):	Graduated June -49.
Mr. I. M. Hale (student):	Graduated. Jun 49.
Mr. Benj. R. Huske (student):	Grad & removed Jun. -50.

_____ **(p. 84)** _____

Communicants
of
the Church in the Parish
of the
Chapel of the Cross
at the Diocesan Convention of 1848–9

*Rev. W. M. Green	Removed to Miss. Dec. 1849
*Mrs. C. J. Green	Removed to Miss. Dec. 1849
*Miss M. W. Green	Removed to Miss. Dec. 1849
Rev. F. M. Hubbard	*Removed, 1868*
Mrs Martha *H.* Hubbard	"
Judge W. H. Battle	"
Mrs Lucy Battle	
Mrs Laura Phillips	Seceded to Presbyterians Sept. – 49
Mrs Rebecca Lucas	
Mrs Hannah Ryan	
Miss Sally S. Mallett	
*Mr John M. Craig	
*Mrs Elizabeth Craig	
*Miss Matilda Williams	
*Mr A. M. Hooper	Removed July -49
Mrs C. Hooper	Removed July 1849
Mr Lloyd Moore	died April 6th 1852
Mr T. D. Haigh (student)	Graduated June. -49
Mr P. M. Hale (student)	Graduated Jun. -49
M^r. Benj. R. Huske (student)	Grad. & removed Jun. -50

_____ (p. 85) _____

Mʳ. S. C. Roberts (student)	Left college
Mr. W. A. Moore (student)	Left college March 1851
Nanny Green (col'd)	Removed to Miss. Dec. 1849
Miss Mary /*Ruffin*/ Smith	*Died 1879*

Added since that time:

Mʳˢ M. A. Ferrell	Removed Aug. 1849
Miss Francenious Ferrell	Do. Do.
Mʳ J. D. Battle	*Removed*
Mʳˢ M. Snipes	
Mʳˢ P. A. Jones	
Mr. Andrew Mickle	Rec'd from Hillsboro' Oct. 1849
Mʳˢ Helen Mickle	Do. Do. Do.
Rev. J. T. Wheat D. D.	Rec'd to this Diocese from Tenn.
Mʳˢ Selina Wheat	Rec'd from Tennessee Jan. 1850
Mʳ J. A. Manning (student)	Left college
Mʳ. Fr. J. Shepard (student)	" "
Mʳ Thomas Hill (student)	removed Nov. 1850
Mr. Richᵈ Hines Jr. (student)	Graduat. and removed Jun. -50
Mr. Lawrence Smith (student)	Do. Do. D.
Miss Sally Williams	
Miss *Susan* C. Battle	
Mʳˢ Mary S. Mallett	
Miss J. May Wheat	Rec'd from Tenn.

Added since Dioces. Convention. May 1850

William Murphy	removed June 1851
Thoˢ Granville Martin	left College Aug. 1850

_____(p. 86) _____

Communicants continued

Mrs. Laura Saunders   Rec'd fr. Ral. July 1850
Jno. T. Wheat Jr.   *Removed*

Added since the Diocesan Convention of 1851

Mr. Edward Mallett (July 6th 3 after Trinity 1851)

  [blank]   Waddell   *1852*
Mrs. [blank]   Jeffries Dec. 5th 1852

Miss Mickle
Mr. Hines
        (Added since Convention '53.)

Mr. Hugh Waddell (Susan H.)   Rec'd from Hillsboro
  "   Henry Waddell (Eliz[h] Blount)   "   "   "
Miss Moore (Sarah Louisa)   "   "   "
Mrs Charlotte Caudle   "   "   Raleigh
  "   Emily Caudle   "   "   "

4 Dec.
Mr. Thomas Paxton   Added 4 Decr. 1853
Mrs. "   Paxton ([blank])   "   "
Miss M. A. McDade   "   "

_____(p. 87) _____

Revised List of Communicants

1.	Rev. F. M. Hubbard	.	Mr. [blank] Waddill
2.	Mrs. Martha Hubbard	.	Mrs. [blank] Jeffries
3.	Judge W. H. Battle	.	Miss [blank] Mickle
4.	Mrs. Lucy <M> Battle	.	Mrs. Susan H. Waddell
5.	" Rebecca Lucas	30.	" Elizabeth B. do. (Remov^d?)
.	" Hannah Ryan	.	Miss Sarah L. Moore
.	Miss Sally S Mallett	.	Mrs. Charlotte Caudle ⎤ Remov^d
.	Mr. John Craig	.	" Emily Caudle ⎦
.	Mrs. Elizabeth Craig	.	Mr. Thomas Paxton
10.	Miss Matilda Williams	35.	Mrs. " Paxton
.	" Mary Smith	.	Miss M. A. McDade
.	[Mrs ... erased]	.	/Dead/ Henry Marsden Waddell
.	" P. A. Jones	.	Alfred Moore Waddell
.	Mr. Andrew Mickle	.	Joseph Bibb Lucas
5.	Mrs Helen Mickle	40.	/(Remove^d)> William Harding Moore
.	Rev. J. T. Wheat	.	John Hines
.	Mrs S. B. Wheat	.	/(Remov^d)/ John Husk Tillinghast
.	Mr. Richd Hines (Remov^d)	.	Mrs. Sarah Fetter
.	Miss Sally Williams	.	/Dec^d/ Delia Smith
20.	" Susan /C./ Battle		(First time on her Death-bed)
.	Mrs. Mary S. Mallett		/Mrs Hunt/
.	" J. May Shober (Remov^d)	5	Mr. Thomas Hill (a Student)
.	" Laura Saunders	.	" [blank] Burton "
.	J. T. Wheat Jr. (Remov^d)		Reported to the convention
5.	Mr. Edward Mallett		of 1855----Remov^d 8
			Dec^d 2
			Present number 36

_____(p. 88) _____

Communicants: Revised List, May 1855

1.	Revd F. M. Hubbard	. .	Mrs. Susan H. Waddell
2.	Mrs. Martha Hubbard	.	Miss Sarah L. Moore
3.	Judge W. H. Battle	.	Mr. Alfred M. Waddell
4.	Mrs. Lucy /M./ Battle	.	Mr. Thomas Paxton
5.	Miss Susan /C./ Battle	.	Mrs. " Paxton
.	Mrs. Rebecca Lucas	.	Mrs. Louisa Hunt
.	" Hannah Ryan	.	Rev^d Dr. Wheat
.	Mr. Joseph /B./ Lucas	.	Mrs. " Wheat
.	Mr. Edward Mallett		(Students)
10.	Mrs. Mary S. Mallett		Mr. Waddill (of Ala.)
.	Miss Sally Mallett		" Hines (of Ral.)
.	Mrs. P. A. Jones		" Burton (of Tenn.)
.	" Laura Saunders	36.	" Hill (of Wilmington)
.	Miss Matilda Williams		" Anderson (of Wilmington)
5.	" Sally Williams		" Johnston (of Edenton)
.	Miss Mary Smith		
.	Mr. Andrew Mickle		
.	Mrs. Helen Mickle		
.	Miss [blank] Mickle		
20.	Mrs. Judge Norwood		
.	" Sarah Fetter		
.	Mr. John Craig		
.	Mrs. Elizabeth Craig		
.	" Jeffries		
25.	Miss McDade		

_____(p. 89)_____

Communicants: Revised List. August 12, 1856

Rev. J. T. Wheat (*Rem.*)

Rev. F. M. Hubbard

Hon. W. H. Battle L.L.D.

Dr Johnston B. Jones

Mr Andrew Mickle

Mr Edward Mallett (Rem^d.)

Mr Charles Mallett

Dr William P Mallett

Mr Joseph Lucas (Dec^d.)

Mr Walker Anderson

M^r [blank] Johnson (*Rem*)

M^r [blank] Stoney (removed.)

M. [blank] Hill (*Rem.*)

M^r [blank] Haigh (*Rem.*)

M^r [blank] Hall (*Rem.*)

   Richardson Mallett.

Mr. James S. Henderson (Rem.)

(Added by rem. since.)

Miss Maria Spear

Mrs Mary Saunders

Miss V. Brandon (*Rem.*)

Mrs. C. Walker (Remov^d)

Miss Elizabeth Mickle

Mrs. Selina Henderson (*Rem.*)

Miss Mary De B. Jones

Mrs Selina Wheat (*Rem. 1859*)

Mrs Martha Hubbard

Mrs Anna K. Lee (Rem^d)

Mrs Lucy /M./ Battle

Mrs Polly Ann Jones

Mrs Rebecca Lucas

Mrs Hannah Ryan

Mrs Mary S. Mallett (Rem^d)

Mrs Laura Saunders

Mrs Helen Mickle

M^{rs} [blank] Norwood (*Rem*)

Mrs. Sarah Fetter

Mrs Louisa Hunt (*Removed*)

Mrs. Sarah Mallet

Mrs Caroline De Berniere Mallett

Miss Sally Mallett

Miss Susan C. Battle

Miss Sally Williams /L *Philip Craig*/

Miss Matilda Williams

Miss Mary Smith

Mrs. Rose Jeffries

Miss Amanda McDade

Miss Ann [blank] Saunders

Miss Martha H. Hubbard

Mrs. /H./ Smith (added)

Mrs. Snipes   "

Mrs. Perkins   "

_____(p. 90) _____

Added 7 Nov.ʳ 1858 by J. T. W. (officiating pro. tem.)

Hildreth /H./ Smith   Leonidas Polk Wheat
Richard /B./ Saunders   Augustus Moore Flythe
Frederick Augustus Fetter   John Routh Bowie
Hugh Hagart Bein   Isaac Augustus Jarratt
Lawrence Mel Anderson   Arthur Nelson McKimmon
Thomas Capehart   George Saunders Martin
Richard Cogdell Badger   George Pettigrew Bryan
Thomas S. Armistead

            Susan Holden (coloured)
                  (61.)

_____(p. 91) _____

List of Communicants 1860 4 [last number crossed out, 0 corrected to 4]

 [The entries in the two columns are in different hands: on the left, Forbes'; on the right, Hilliard's]

Rev F *M* Hubbard

Mrs *M H* Hubbard

Miss M Hubbard

Hon Wm Battle

Mrs *Lucy M.* Battle

Miss *Susan* /*C.*/ Battle

Mr. Junius /*C*/ Battle   [in margin:] died 1862

Mr A Mickle

Mrs [blank] Mickle

Miss E Mickle

Mr C P Mallett

Mrs [blank] Mallett

Mr Richard/*son*/ Mallett [in margin:] died 1863

Miss M Mallett

Dr. Wm /*P*/ Mallett

Mrs /*Caroline*/ Mallett

Miss Eliza Mallett

Miss Sallie Mallett

Mrs F Mallett – [in margin:] removed

Miss Lissie Mallett– [in margin:] removed

Mrs M. Fetter

Mr F Fetter

Prof H Smith

Mrs H Smith

Mrs Margaret Smith– [in margin:] removed]

Miss Mary Smith

Mr. T. M. Argo

Mrs. F. W. Hilliard

Joseph Mickle

1st June 1862 Mrs. Wm. Van Wyck Jr

Miss Lydia Van Wyck

Communed 1st time 17th May 1862

Annie Mickle

Sophy Mallett

Communed 1st time 1st June '62

Mrs. Mary J. Van Wyck

Wm. Lowndes Quarles removed

Communed 1st time 8th June '62

Albert M. Boozer

Communed 1st time 7th Sept. 1862

Nancy Perkins

Communed 1st time 28th March '63

Thos M. Argo

Augustus Van Wyck

Lucy Whitaker — removed

Albina Mears (col'd) removed

Communed first time (here) 8th Aug '63

Mrs. Ellen Person - removed

_____(p. 92) _____

List of Communicants 1860 4 the heading and names are in Forbes' hand; the last digit is crossed out and 0 corrected to 4]

Dr J. Jones
Mrs J Jones
Miss M Jones
Miss Maria L. Spear   removed
Mr George Johnston   died May 7th 1864
Mrs "   Johnston   *(by removal) since Convention* [entry in Hilliard's hand]
Mr. R W Anderson   removed
Mr George Bryan removed
Mrs. Lucas
Mrs Bryan
Miss Bryan *(By first communion)*
Mrs. Laura Saunders
Mrs Richard Saunders
Miss A Saunders
Mr J Saunders
Mr Gesner   removed
Miss Sallie Williams
Miss M. Williams
Mrs Geffries
Miss A McDade
Mrs Perkins

Students
Com. 1860
Mr. G. Johnston ~~rem~~
T. S. Armistead
H Graham removed
J Haughton removed
T Capeheart removed
J Mallett removed

Susan Holden Colored

_____(p. 93) _____

[the lists are entirely in Hilliard's hand]

Communed 1st time 11th Aug. 1863 (here)
  Thomas Harvey – dead

Communed 1st time 26th April 1864
  Lydia Van Wyck – removed – June –1864
  Kate Fetter –
  Florence Wright –
  Robena Mickle
  S. Garland Ryan
  John S. Henderson
  Herbert Mallett –
  Wm A. Wright Jr
  Henry A London Jr
  David Moore (Free Colored)
  Cornelius Burnet   "

Communed 1st time May 1864 (Ascension)
  Iredell Johnston

Added at Various times
Mrs. F. W. Hilliard
Mrs. Sarah A. Hill -
Mrs. Fanny Morrow -
Miss Cox -
Miss Annie Swain -
Miss Ella Swain -
Prof. John Kimberly -
Mrs. Betty Kimberly –

_____(p. 94) _____

Communicants 1864-
    Added at various times –
Mr. E. H. Davis
Mrs. E. H. Davis
Mrs. Mears
Mrs. John De Rossett-
Mrs. H. G. Spruill-
Miss Eva Spruill-
Mr. Wm K. Davis-
Mrs. Wm K. Davis-
Mrs. Jane Ward
Miss Peters-
Rev. Dr. S. I. Johnston-
Mrs. "   "   "   (Margaret Ann)
Miss Helen S. Johnston-
Mr. John Johnston-
Mr. Albert R. Elliot-
Mrs. "   "   " (Juliana)
Mrs. Thos Hamey (Mary) -
Joseph A. Mickle -
Edward Gregory Prout -
William C. Prout -
Emma (col^d) serv^t of Miss Mary Smith –
_____   "   "   "   "   "   "

Mr. Chalmers - removed
Mr. J. Chalmers   removed

Communed 1st time Whitsunday 15th May 1864
Eliza - Servt of Ch. P. Mallett --

_____(p. 95) _____

Communed 1ˢᵗ time - 5th June - 1864
Susan Fetter - (Confirmed at St Mary's School Raleigh - 1ˢᵗ May 1864)

Communed 1ˢᵗ time – 3ʳᵈ July 1864
Andrew Perkins
Laura (Servᵗ of Miss Mary Smith)

Virginius St. Clair McNider – Sept. 3ʳᵈ 1865

Miss Susan Davis – Aug. 1867

List of Communicants Revised May 13ᵗʰ 1876

Miss Mary R. Smith
"   Maria L. Spear
Mrs. Laura Saunders
Miss Ann Saunders
Mrs. Sarah Taylor
        James Taylor
        Isaac Taylor   removed 1877   *Mistake—refers to James /Taylor/ whose removal was only*
                                                            temporary

        Andrew Mickle
Mrs. Helen M. Mickle
Miss Annie W. Mickle   removed 1877
        Robina N. Mickle   removed 1877
        Jane T. Mickle   died Feb. 20th 1878
        Lizzie B. Mickle
Prof. J. DeB. Hooper
Mrs Mary Hooper
Miss Julia Hooper

Dr Wm P. Mallett
Mrs DeBerniere Mallett
Miss Sophia Mallett
"   Eliza Mallett
Mrs Susan Barbee
Mrs Margaret B. Davis
Prof. John J. Kimberly   Removed to Asheville 1876
Mrs Mary Saunders
          Students
Robert Davis of Louisburg   left college Dec. 77
Francis Winston
[blank] Griffin   left college 1877
Richard Henderson   left [erased?]
Kemp P. Battle Jr.   *Resides at Chapel Hill*
John M. Manning   1st communion Jan. 20th 1878
Jas S. Manning   1st "   "   20th 1878
Robert Strange   1st "   "   "   "
Ernest Haywood   1st "   "   "   "
James /H./ Ruffin   1st "   "   "   "
Frank Wood   Left college May 1878
Hugh Davis   "   "
H. Lutterloh
A. M. Waddell Jr   Left College
John Walker
Lucien Walker

_____(p. 97) _____

Mrs. Rosanna Jeffries /Rowe/ by Removal from Raleigh Jan. 1877   Removed June 78
Miss Sue Jeffries   "   "   "   " "   "   "   "
  "   Mary Amanda McDade   "   "   " "   "   "   "
Hon. Wm H. Battle   "   "   "   1877   Died Mch. 14th 1879
Pres^t Kemp P. Battle   "   "   "   "
Mrs. (Pattie) /Martha A./ Battle   "   "   "   "
Miss Lena Foust   "   Pittsboro Jan 1878
Mrs Helen Wills   "   from Willson
    James Wills   "   "   "
Miss Ann Munroe   "   "   Raleigh 1878
Thomas H. Battle   by removal from Raleigh in 1877 but not heretofore recorded
Mrs Annie Huske Cheshire by removal from Tarboro 1878
Miss Laura B. Saunders, by first communion Apl. 30th 1879
    Rumbough, Henry   by removal to University from Madison County NC
    Haigh, Jno. DeLagnel   "   "   "   "   Fayetteville
    Skinner, Frederick Nash "   "   "   "   Edenton
    Peebles, Henry Bruce   "   "   "   "   Northampton County N.C.
    Albertson, Robt. Brook "   "   "   "   Perquimans County N.C.
    Fenner Stickney   "   "   "   "   Pitt County   Removed Ap. 79

_____(p. 98) _____

List of Communicants in the Parish May 19th 1878

Hon. Wm H. Battle	Died Mch 14th 1879
" Kemp P. Battle	
Mrs. Martha A. Battle	
Kemp P. Battle Jr.	student
Thos H. Battle	student
Miss Mary R Smith	
Maria L. Spear	died Jany. 5th 1881
Mrs. Laura Saunders	
/Mrs. Mary Saunders/	
Miss Ann Saunders	
Miss Laura B. Saunders	added by First Communion April 30th 1879
Mrs. Sarah Taylor	
James /C./ Taylor	removed to New York, Jany 1880
Isaac /M./ Taylor	
Andrew Mickle	
Mrs. Helen M. Mickle	
Miss Lizzie /B./ Mickle	
Prof. J. DB. Hooper	
Mrs. Mary Hooper	
Mrs. Julia Hooper Graves	
Dr. William P. Mallet	
Mrs. DeBernier Mallet	
Miss Eliza Mallet	
" Sophia Mallet	Removed March 1880 to Jackson. N.Hampton Co.
Mrs. Susan Barbee	

_____(p. 99) _____

Communicants

Mrs. Margaret B Davis
Mrs. Rosanna Jeffries Rowe ⎤ Removed
Miss Mary Amanda McDade ⎦ June 1878
  "   Lena Foust
    James Wills
Mrs. Helen Wills
Miss Ann Monroe   died Oct. 29th 1880
Miss Annie Huske Cheshire   by removal /from Tarboro/ June 1878
Miss Martha G. Mallett   removed to Hickory N.C. Nov. 1878

Students in the University

Francis /D/ Winston   <u>May 1879 withdrawn</u>
Richard /B./ Henderson Removed <u>June 1879</u>
Jno. M. Manning   do.   do.
Jas. S. Manning   do.   do.
Robert Strange   do.   do.
Ernest Haywood   do.   <u>June 1880</u> to Raleigh
James H. Ruffin
Frank Wood   /lost/ Removed June /or May/ 1878
Hugh L. Davis   do.   "
Herbert Latterloh   do.   "   1880
John M. Walker
Lucien H. Walker
Henry Rumbough /gained/ By removal Sept. 1878
John DeLagnel Haigh "   do. "   "

_____(p. 100) _____

Communicants

Robert Brook Albertson	/gained/ by removal	Sept. 1878
Henry Bruce Peebles	" " "	"
Fred. Nash Skinner	" "	January 1879
Fenner Stickney	" "	Sept. 1878 <u>lost</u> by removal Ap. 1879

[???] May 14th 1879: <u>Forty-Three</u>

Frank B. Dancy (by first communion in Tarboro) June 15th 1879
Joseph Carey Dowd   "   "   "   "   "   removed Dec. 1879
Herbert B. Battle   added by first Communion July 6th 1879
Walter E. Philips   do.   do. Sept. 28th 1879
Henry L. Battle   do.   do. do.   "   removed Dec. '80
Francis G. Hines   do.   do. do.   "
Chas. Watts Smedes   do.   by Removal from   Raleigh Sept. 1879
Evert Bancker Smedes   do.   do.   "   do.   "   "
William Cobb Whitfield   do.   do.   Lenoir County Jany. 1880
Zeno Brown   do. by first communion Feb. 8th Quinq. Sunday 1880.
Elizabeth Brandon Saunders, by first Communion Nov. 9th. 1879
Herbert W. Pender, student, by first communion Apl. 18th 1880
Hunter Sharp, student, from Hertford County, Feb. 1880

May 26th 1880. <u>51</u>
<u>Fifty-One</u>

Wm Lowndes Heune, from Brevard, Transylvania Co., Sept. 1880
Robina N. Mickle, from Texas, Aug. 1880
Hannah S. Doury, from [blank]
/James Cole/ Roberts (student)
Mrs. [blank] Adney, expecting & desiring confirmation has /was/ admitted to
the Holy Communion on Easter Day 1881.

_____(p. 101) _____

Communicants at Mission Station at Durham.
April 1880 —

	Robert F. Webb	
	Mrs. Henrietta J. Webb	
	Wm L. Wall	

Robert F. Webb
Mrs. Henrietta J. Webb
Wm L. Wall
Mrs. Catharine S. Wall
Spencer W. Chamberlain
Mrs. Olivia [blank] Chamberlain
Charles M. Herndon
Mrs. M. P. Raiford
Mrs. Alexina G. Barham
Mrs. Claude B. Hooker
Miss Maggie Palmer
Wm H. Disosway   Removed to Oxford, Aug. 1880
Henry M. Rosemond
Mrs. D. C. Mangam
Mrs. [blank] Poe   dead
Mrs. Mary E. Smith
Miss Annie E. Wampler
Miss Lena Morris Wampler
Cornelia Fitzgerald (colored)
Miss Sallie Williams.   May 26th 1880. Twenty (20)
Johnson Ward   removed to Ohio & gone to the bad

First Com. Aug. 1 -80   James N. Gammon
"   "   "   Josephine S. Gammon
"   "   "   Dora P. Rosemond
"   "   Oct. 3^d 1880   Claude C. Barham
Oct. 1880 from Md.   Mrs. Kate N. Wampler
"   "   Julia Cummings Wampler

_____(p. 102) _____

Communicants at Durham – continued

Mrs. Sarah Hanks	Jany. 1881	from	Ringwood
" Agnes Sandford	Mch. 1881	"	Fayetteville
" Ade Cook	1880		
Gardner	Mch. 1881	"	Raleigh
Mrs. [blank] Gardner	" "	"	"
Robert Ransom Jr.	" 1881	from	New Bern
Mrs. Sarah M. Mallory	May 1881	"	Pittsboro
Miss Catharine Fowler	Apl. 1881	"	Chatham County
Mrs. [blank] Anderson	May 1881	"	Greensboro
Alfred R. Bradeen		"	A

Miss. [blank] Ledger (colored teacher)

_____(pp. 103-111 blank) _____

_____(p. 112) _____

Families	1849-50
Rev. Prof. Hubbard's:	
Rev. Prof. Wheat's:	
Judge Battle's:	
Mr. Mickle's:	
Mrs. Lucas':	
Miss S. Mallett's:	
Dr Jones':	
Mr Craig's:	
Prof. Fetter's:	
Mrs Ferrell's:	Removed 1849
Rev. Dr Green's:	Removed 1849
Mr. Ed. J. Mallett's:	
Mrs Laura Saunders:	Rec'd from Raleigh July 1850
Mr. Hugh Waddell	" " Hillsboro 1853
Mrs. Sutherland	
Mr. Paxton	

_____(p. 113 blank) _____

_____(p. 114) _____

1st page

Collections, Offertory, & Disbursements by the Rector

1856	Colls etc			1856	Disbmts	
Mar. 2	Offertory	$ 5.00		April 1	Bill of Books from T. N. Stanford N York	$19.90
Mar. 23	Easter Sunday for Sunday School	17.86		"	½ Freight on do.	3.25
April.	Additional subscriptions by Mr R. Battle $1 Children of Dr. Jones /.45 ea/	1.45		Apr. 7	Clothes for Andw Perkins	1.80
Apr. 13	Communion Alms	4.73		July 27	Coll. for Dioc. Miss. by Bp. A	11.50
" 17.	/fr./ Mr Lucas for Mr Wetmore for SS	1.00		Aug. 12	Donation to Mrs Perkins	2.00
July 6	Communion Alms	3.40		Aug. 16	Funeral Expenses of Child of Mrs. P	3.00
July 27	Coll. for Dio. Miss. by Bishop A.	11.50		Aug. 17	Paid Sexton	2.00
Aug. 10	Communion Alms	3.55		Nov. 2	" "	2.00
Sep. 7	Communion Alms	3.68		Oct. 4	Books for Sunday School	10.00
Oct. 5	Communion Alms	6.15		/1857/ Jan. 20	Remitted to Treas. Dom. Miss.	17.00
Nov. 2	Communion Alms	5.00		Apr. 18	Paid Sexton	2.00
/1857/ Jan. 4	Offertory for Domes. Missions	15.00		May 1	2 prs. Shoes for S. S. children	2.20
" "	Additional: for same	2.00		" 5	Remitted to Treas. For. Miss.	27.00
Feb. 1	Communion Alms	6.30		" 6	Books & Cards for S. S	14.40
Mar. 1	Offertory for For. Mis.	15.68		Sep. 5	Shoes for S. Scholars	2.65
" "	Night Coll. for Same	11.32		" 6	Paid Sexton	3.00
Apr. 12	Easter Offerings	4.72		" 7	Bal. of Books for SS as pr. Stat.	6.75
May 3	Communion Alms	4.56		Oct. 4	Paid Sexton	1.00
May 31	Whitsunday offerings	5.50		Nov	Sundry charities (shoes. clothes etc.)	5.00

July 5	Communion Alms	3.16	" 16	Amt. app'd for Mrs Perkins & children's clothes	3.50
Aug. 2	Communion Alms	6.50	Dec. 8	Wood for same	2.50
July 19	Offs. for Af. Miss. by Cornelia servant /girl of Miss M. Smith/	.25c	" "	Remitted to Treas. Dom. Miss.	31.65
Sep. 6	Communion Alms	6.75	" 25	Christmas Tree /½/ for S. S.	3.00
Oct. 4	Communion Alms	3.84	" 28	Medicines for Mrs. P.	1.50
Nov. 1	Communion Alms	4.80	" 30	Paid Owen for Sexton (1 pr boots)	2.75
Dec. 6	Advent offering for Dom. Miss.	31.65	1858 Aug. 18	Paid Sexton (which balances these columns)	4.00

_____(p. 115)_____

Collections etc. Continued

1858			1858		
Jan. 3	Communion Alms	$5.36	Jan. 23	Paid Sexton	$5.00
" -	Addinal Contributions for Dom. Miss.	4.50	" -	Remitted to Dom. Comn	$4.50
Feb. 7	Collection for For. Missins	31.35	Feb. 27	Remitted to For. Missns by Mr. Mickle	31.35
Mar. 7	Communion Alms	3.20	Mar. 7	Paid Sexton	2.00
Apr. 4 /Easter/	Offerings	7.33	Mar. 10	Provisions for Mrs Perkins	1.50
May 2	Communion Alms	6.00	Apr. 17	Paid Sexton	3.00
Aug. 1	Offertory	4.00	" 20	Meal for Mrs P.	.80
			May 4	Paid Sexton	2.50
			"	Music Books	4.50
			Aug. 9	Paid Corpn Tax on Rectory	2.50
			" 21	Cash received from Rev. H. T. Lee which balances the account	4.09

Due Sexton for
  first two years   *14.25*
   Due some for last ½ *<u>1.50</u>*
                 15.75
This amt. is due from
  the Church—
Paid Sex. by the Treas:
    $3.00
leaving a balance
     due him of
    $12.75
        H. T. Lee
          Rector

——————————(p. 116)——————————

1852 -- 1-53
Sund. $6.55   *$29.41*

<u>Acc^t of Collections & Attendance at Com'n</u>

		Attend.	$ cts.			At.	$ cts.
1853	February 6th	14	2.65	1854	February 5th	22	3.87½
"	March 6	13	2.65				
"	Easter	20	6.08				
"	May 1st	19	<u>4.55</u>				
			$ 15.93				
"	August	17	4.80				
"	September	20	5.25				
"	October 2nd	25	6.00				
"	November 6th	22	6.50				
"	December 4th	31	9.50				
Since last Convention			$32.05				

	$ cts		$ cts
1859 August 7th	7.19	Sexton	1.00
Sep 4th	9.35	Work	.95
Oct 2	8.25	Poor	.95
Nov 6	8.65	Sexton 1.75 Lock .35	2.10
Nov Bishop's visit	20.00	Communion wine Oct.1859	4.62 ½
Dec Christmas	24.00	Sunday school Books	5.22
1860 Jan 29th	9.65	Clothes for Poor	1.80
March 4th	10.70	Poor 3.90 Poor 1.00 $4.80	9.70
April Easter (8th)	12.55	To the Bishop	20.00
		Miss cond	24.00
May (absent)			
June 3rd	_11.60_	Poor 50, 1.65, 1.00, 3.40, 2.30	8.85
	121.44	Locks 1.15, Clothes for Poor 4.60	5.75
July 1st	5.65	Work for the Church 1.25, .50	1.75
August	7.25	Poor 4.00, 6.69	10.69
September	8.44	Plastering Columns & Buttresses	5.00
October	_7.50_	Chains for the gates	1.35
	150.28	MM account of Mrs. Perkins	11.37 ½
	_145.40_		_120.11_
Balance given to Mrs. Hutton for Mrs Perkins	4.88	Sexton 1.50, 2.50, 1.50	5.50
		Poor 1.50, 5.39, 4.50, 6.00	17.39
		Sexton 1.50 poor .90	_2.40_
			145.40
E. M. Forbes			

123

_____(p. 117) _____

[The page has a number of different calculations noted down, unidentified, and the following sums:]

Com. Coll.	9.00	at the Offertory	46.82 ½
Bell	26.45	Choir for Seraphim [?]	91.50
Altar Cloth	5.00	Comm. Set fr 4 persons	35.00
		Fr. missions Paroch. p...	2.50
		Gen. Dom. Miss.	20.05
		For. " "	16.12 ½

212.00

Collections
 at
Communions

1853
Feb. 6 $2.65
March 6.   2.65
Easter   6.08
May 1   4.55
            15.93

_____(p. 118) _____

[the following handwritten document is tipped onto a page headed *R. S. McRae, Chapel Hill, NC*]

At a meeting of the Vestry of the Parish of the Chapel of the Cross held the 16th day of November AD 1868.

It was resolved

1ˢᵗ That we the Vestry of the Parish of the Chapel of the Cross, on behalf of ourselves and the Congregation of the Parish, do sincerely /regret/ the Necessity which severs our Connection with our respected Pastor, the Revᵈ Fordyce M Hubbard DD.

2ᵈ. That for his almost gratuitous service to the Parish in its Condition of impoverishment Caused by the late War, he is entitled to, and we hereby tender him, our most gratefull thanks and acknowledgements

3ᵈ. That he and his family have our kindest wishes and our prayers for their wellfare and happiness in their future of this life, as well as that beyond the grave,

4. That a Copy of these resolutions be sent to the Revᵈ Dʳ Hubbard, and that they be entered by the Clerk of the Vestry on the records of the Parish.

_____(p. 119 = back board) _____

Oct. 1843   *Preached Funeral Sermon of Mʳˢ Rebecca Cameron*

Oct. 1843   *Preached Funeral sermon of Col. Herbert Sims*

Mem.   *[pencil entries too faint to read—3? lines]*

Mem.   *Minna (colored infant) of Mason & Sarah*
            Minny (do.   ) of Simon & Rilla
         all the property of Duncan Cameron, baptized at John Chapel by Rev W M Green,
         April 11ᵗʰ 1847

BIBLIOGRAPHY

Battle, Kemp P., *History of the University of North Carolina*, vol. 1 (Raleigh: Edwards and Broughton, 1907); vol. 2 1 (Raleigh: Edwards and Broughton, 1912).

Battle, Kemp Plummer, *Memories of an Old-time Tar Heel* (Chapel Hill: UNC Press, 1945).

Battle, Kemp P., *Sketch of the Life and Character of Wilson Caldwell* (Chapel Hill: University Press Company, 1895).

Chamberlain, Hope Summerell, *Old Days in Chapel Hill* (Chapel Hill: UNC Press, 1926).

Chapman, John K. (Yonni), "Black Freedom and the University of North Carolina, 1793–1960" (doctoral dissertation, University of North Carolina, 2006).

Edes, Grace Williamson, *Annals of the Harvard College Class of 1852* (Cambridge, MA: privately printed, 1922).

Fox-Genovese, Elizabeth, *Within the Plantation Household: Black and White Women of the Old South* (Chapel Hill: UNC Press, 1988).

Franklin, John Hope, *The Free Negro in North Carolina, 1790–1860* (Chapel Hill: UNC Press, 1943).

Gass, W. Conard, "A Felicitous Life: Lucy Martin Battle, 1805–1874," *The North Carolina Historical Review*, 52 (1975), 367–93.

Graebner, N. Brooks, "The Episcopal Church and Race in Nineteenth-Century North Carolina," *Anglican and Episcopal History* 78 (2009), 85–93.

Graebner, N. Brooks, "'Hitherto excluded for want of room': Slave evangelization in the North Carolina ministry of William Mercer Green from 1823 to 1848." Paper presented at the Natchez Historical Association, October 9, 2009.

Harper, C. W., "House Servants and Field Hands: Fragmentation in the Antebellum Slave Community," *The North Carolina Historical Review* 55 (1978), 42–59.

Henderson, Archibald, *The Church of the Atonement and the Chapel of the Cross at Chapel Hill, North Carolina* (Hartford, CT.: Church Missions Publishing Company, June–August 1938).

Johnson, Guion Griffis, *Ante-bellum North Carolina: A Social History* (Chapel Hill: UNC Press, 1937).

Jones, H. G., *Miss Mary's Money: Fortune and Misfortune in a North Carolina Plantation Family, 1760–1924* (Jefferson, NC: McFarland, 2015).

Lefler, Hugh, and Paul Wager, eds., *Orange County—1752–1952* (Chapel Hill: privately published, 1953).

London, Laurence Foushee, and Sarah McCulloh Lemmon, eds., *The Episcopal Church in North Carolina, 1701–1959* (Raleigh: The Episcopal Diocese of North Carolina, 1987).

MacNider, William de Berniere, *The Good Doctor* (Chapel Hill: UNC Press, 1953).

Malone, E. T., Jr., *The Episcopal Church in North Carolina During the War Between the States* (Warrenton, NC: Literary Lantern Press, 2013).

Murray, Pauli, *Proud Shoes* (New York: Harper, 1956).

Othow, Helen Chavis, *John Chavis: African American Patriot, Preacher, Teacher, and Mentor, 1763–1838* (Jefferson, NC: McFarland, 2001).

Raper, Horace W., *William W. Holden: North Carolina's Political Enigma* (Chapel Hill and London: UNC Press, 1985).

Rees, Philip A., "The Chapel of the Cross: An Architectural History" (M.A. thesis, University of North Carolina, 1979).

Smith, Kim, "Book of Harriet: The Disambiguation of Five North Carolinian Siblings 1840–1941" (Master's Project, Master of Arts in Liberal Studies, Duke University, 2016).

Snider, William D., *Light on the Hill* (Chapel Hill and London: UNC Press, 1992).

Spencer, Cornelia Phillips, "A Notable Woman North Carolina Has Produced," *State Chronicle* (Raleigh), February 28, 1886, p. 1; reprinted in Spencer, *Selected Papers*, 710–14.

Spencer, Cornelia Phillips, "Pen and Ink Sketches of the U.N.C." (typewritten copy of articles in the Raleigh *Sentinel*, 1869), Special Collections, Wilson Library, University of North Carolina.

Spencer, Cornelia Phillips, *Selected Papers*, ed. Louis R. Wilson (Chapel Hill: UNC Press, 1953).

Waddell, Alfred Moore, *Stories of My Life* (Raleigh: Edwards and Broughton, 1908).

Wright, Annette C., "The 'Grown-up Daughter': The Case of North Carolina's Cornelia Phillips Spencer," *The North Carolina Historical Review* 74 (1997), 260–83.

INDEXES OF NAMES

The COTC register records the activities of over 600 named persons, a sizable fraction of Chapel Hill's population at that time, free and enslaved, of about 2000, though of course that 600-plus includes many visitors and university students. In identifying these names with particular individuals, I inevitably learned more about them than just their full names, and it seemed to me that an index of names that supplied some of that other information might help convey a better picture, not only of that little community, but also of the wider (but still small) one of which it was a part. So in many index entries I have made note of family relationships, and UNC students have been distinguished by an (S) after their names. Page references in bold face are to the introduction; the remainder are to the register itself. I apologize in advance for the mistakes and mis-identifications that I am sure still exist.

As I went about trying to provide close identifications, it became clear to me that our intermittent string of rectors did not always hear accurately the names of occasional visitors to the parish, and indeed did not consistently agree on the spelling of those of their regular parishioners. There is thus great variability in the spelling of the names of the same individual as set down in the register: Mrs. [Rose] Jeffries, for example, also appears as Mrs. "Jeffreys" and Mrs. "Geffries"; Susan and George Chavis are recorded as "Chavers". This index enters names under the spelling used in contemporary sources of record (e.g., the U.S. Census) or authoritative sources like the *Alumni History of the University of North Carolina*, but my transcription of the core register always reports the original spelling in the manuscript, and the index adds that spelling parenthetically as well. In many cases a precise identification of a person was impossible, and I have entered them under their surnames but have maintained the prefixes used in the register (Miss, Mrs., Mr.) so as at least to make clear their civil style.

The purpose of a name index is obviously to make it easy to search for particular individuals. About 15% of the individuals named in our register were enslaved persons, and it has been difficult to know how best to make their names searchable, given that in that society they were considered not to have last names and were often casually identified by their owner's name. In the end, I decided to index their appearance in the register in two ways. Thus William Mercer Green's enslaved house-servant, Nanny Green, will be found in the General Index entered alphabetically (slightly indented) as [Green,] Nanny, together with the rest of the Green family. But she will also be found under her given name in the separate alphabetical Index of Enslaved Persons that follows, as Nanny [Green]. References to formerly enslaved persons who appear in our register after emancipation are entered into the general index under their [new?] surnames. I hope that this combination of approaches will make it as easy as possible for future family researchers to identify such individuals.

GENERAL INDEX

Adney, Mrs., 116

Albertson, Robert Brooke (S), 113, 116

Anderson, Mrs., 118

Anderson, Lawrence Mel (S), **27**, 81, 106

Anderson, Robert Walker (S), **16, 27**, 69, 104, 105, 108

Archer, Millie N., **18n**

Argo, Thomas M. (s.-in-law of F. M. Hubbard), 82, 88, 107

Armistead, Robert, 61

Armistead, Thomas Stewart (s. of Robert) (S), 61, 81, 106, 108

Atkins, Eleanor H. (Mrs. S. D.), 87. *See also* Swain

Atkins, Smith D., 87

Atkinson, Thomas (Bishop), **13, 15, 32, 33, 34, 38, 49**, 70, 78–83 passim, 120

Badger, Richard Cogdell (S), 81, 106

Barbee, Sarah, 97

Barbee, Mrs. Susan M., 96, 112, 114

Barham, Alexina G. (Mrs. C. A. W.), 75, 117

Barham, Claude C., 117

Barham, Claude Virginia Claypoole, 78

Barham, Claudius A. W., 75

Barham, Jethro (s. of C. A. W.), 75

[Battle], Ann Elisa, 67

Battle], Annie Swain, 67

[Battle], Chancy, 67

[Battle], Cora, 72

Battle, Cornelia Viola (d. of K. P.) *See* Lewis, C. V.

[Battle], Edward Plummer, 67

[Battle], Fanny Green, 67

[Battle], Henry, **34, 47**, 67, 88

Battle, Henry Laurence (s. of J. J.) (S), 74, 78, 116

Battle, Herbert Bemerton (s. of K. P.) (S), 78, 116

[Battle], Horace, 67

[Battle], Isabella, 67

[Battle], Jane, **45**, 67, 86,

Battle, Joel Dossey (s. of W. H.), 62, 79, 101

Battle, Joseph John, 74

[Battle], Judy, **45, 50**, 67, 87

Battle, Junius Cullen (s. of W. H.), 81, 107

Battle, Kemp Plummer (s. of W. H.) (S), **2, 4n, 8–9, 14–15, 20, 36n, 39n, 42, 43, 50**, 66, 73, 74, 89, 96, 113, 114

Battle, Kemp Plummer, Jr. (S), 74, 112, 114

Battle, Laura Caroline (sister of W. H.), 60, 86. *See also* Phillips

[Battle], Lizzy (Lissy) Morphis, **45**, 67, 86

Battle, Lucy Martin (Plummer) (Mrs. W. H.), **8, 45–48 passim**, 60–67 passim, 100, 103–107

[Battle], Margaret, 67

Battle, Martha Ann (Mrs. K. P.), 73, 74, 113, 114

Battle, Mary Johnston (d. of W. H.; Mrs. Wm. van Wyck, Jr.), 60, 88

Battle, Mr. R., 118

[Battle], Patsy Alice, 67

Battle, Richard Henry (s. of W. H.), 60

[Battle], Robert Lewis, 72

[Battle], Rufus, 67

Battle, Susan Catharine (d. of W. H.), **8, 46**, 62, 67, 79, 94, 101–107 passim

[Battle], Sylla, 67

Battle, Thomas Hall (s. of K. P.) (S), 114

[Battle], Washington, 72

Battle, Wesley Lewis (s. of W.H.), 60

Battle, William Horn, **5, 8–9, 12, 20, 21n, 32, 34, 35n, 36n, 37, 39n, 40–47, 50**, 60, 62, 64, 66, 72, 73, 88, 92, 93, 94, 100, 103–107 passim, 113, 114, 119

Beatty, Charles, 88

Bein, Hugh Hagart (S), 81, 106

INDEX OF ENSLAVED PERSONS

Editor's Biography

MICHAEL MCVAUGH grew up in Ann Arbor, MI, where his father was on the botany faculty of the University of Michigan. He met his wife-to-be while a Harvard undergraduate majoring in History of Science; they married after he entered the Princeton graduate program in that subject and joined All Saints' parish there. When he joined the UNC history faculty in 1964 and moved to Chapel Hill, they transferred their membership to the Chapel of the Cross, where he became the archivist in the 1990s. He retired from teaching in 2007, but has continued to publish his researches into the history of early science.

After coming to UNC he became fascinated with the role of science in the nineteenth-century university, and especially in the career of Elisha Mitchell, who taught geology and other sciences there from 1818 to 1857. In studying Mitchell's library and papers, he came upon Mitchell's manuscript journal of botanical explorations in Orange County; he enlisted his father's aid, and the two of them used it to reconstruct Mitchell's plant discoveries and to identify the localities where they were made. Their researches were published in 1996. That first engagement with local history led him to appreciate the richness of this parish register as a witness to early Chapel Hill.